D CLAUDE EBUSSY

CLASSIC *f*M LIFELINES

D CLAUDE EBUSSY

AN ESSENTIAL GUIDE TO HIS LIFE AND WORKS

JONATHON BROWN

PAVILION

First published in Great Britain in 1996 by
PAVILION BOOKS LIMITED
26 Upper Ground, London SE1 9PD

Copyright © Pavilion Books Ltd 1996
Front cover illustration © The Hulton Deutsch Collection 1996

Edited and designed by Castle House Press, Llantrisant, South Wales
Cover designed by Bet Ayer

A CIP catalogue record for this book is available
from the British Library

ISBN 1 85793 972 7

Set in Lydian and Caslon
Printed and bound in Great Britain by Mackays of Chatham

2 4 6 8 10 9 7 5 3 1

This book can be ordered direct from the publisher.
Please contact the Marketing Department.
But try your bookshop first.

Contents

A NOTE FROM THE EDITORS

A biography of this type inevitably contains numerous references to pieces of music. The paragraphs are also peppered with 'quotation marks', since much of the tale is told through reported speech.

Because of this, and to make things more accessible for the reader as well as easier on the eye, we decided to simplify the method of typesetting the names of musical works. Conventionally this is determined by the nature of the individual work, following a set of rules whereby some pieces appear in italics, some in italics and quotation marks, others in plain roman type and others still in roman and quotation marks.

In this book, the names of all musical works are simply set in italics. Songs and arias appear in italics and quotation marks.

ACKNOWLEDGMENTS

I am very conscious of the way in which a Chopinesque performance in Edinburgh of one of the books of *Préludes*, given by Roy
Howat, a Debussy scholar apart from anything else, followed by
a fascinating conversation a couple of days later, had a distinct
effect on my hitherto carelessly hazy way of listening to Debussy.
It is a pleasure to be able here to signal that I have not forgotten
that.

Nor have I forgotten the earlier sequence of letters and
conversations with Professor Robert Gibson of the University of
Kent at Canterbury, during the many seasons I spent working on
the novelist Alain-Fournier. It is not quite so directly relevant,
but Fournier, who was present at the premiere of *Pelléas et Mélisande* and in whom that opera was thereafter ever present, gave
me a surrogate nostalgia for the Paris that was home to Debussy
too, and Robert Gibson gave me sanity when dottiness diverted
me.

On a more directly practical level I must thank my sister for
sending out books I needed, as well as Thomas Spronken for
fiddling with wires and plugs and things and for biffing the
modem at the right point with the right weight. And Hilary
Spronken for putting up with us the while. Everyone at Castle
House Press has put up with me generously and I am grateful for
what I shall think of as the pruning, weeding and watering
required. And Peggy Donnelly, for seeing that the hi-fi didn't go
the way of the fridge.

Talking of Paris, I owe more than I can say to Lisbeth and the
famille Songeur for their love and support, as well as to Cécile
Perrin, for love and the subjunctive.

The twentieth century has seen some of the values of inti-
macy in music put to one side in favour of textures and complexity, both of which, however fine, fabulous or fantastic they be, can
also be just a little frightening. Debussy loved to be fascinated by
the ironic strength in small things, in delicate glimpses, by
intimation of a gentle hand at work. He was aware of the gloomy
alternative. I should like to dedicate this book to the memory of
Henry Geldzahler, who also noticed such things.

PRÉLUDE . . .
DEBUSSY THIS WAY AND THAT

My copy of *Debussy: Impressionism & Symbolism* by Stefan Jarocinski was bought second-hand at an age at which such things
can seem important; the previous owner had annotated it
liberally in a pencil ever more blunt as one page turns over to the
next and in writing ever more exasperated: 'Le grand twaddle
français' is his or her remark at the close of the preface (by one
Vladimir Jankélévitch). Elsewhere there is 'crass' and 'what a
bore' as well as 'culture-trip cliché stuff' and 'heavy-goingness',
intermingled with one moment of agreement: 'Yes, yes, but why
go on about it?'

Indeed. I had never had any idea that Debussy could inspire
such rage. Or confusion. Or at any rate that he did so still. Proust
wrote of his impression that *Le Martyre de Saint Sébastien*, a piece
written by Debussy in 1911, was punctuated by what sounded
like 'farts'. True, in his day Debussy did inspire rage or anger or
despair but then that was in the vapid and posturing world of *bel
époque* and pre-war France; what else does one expect? – there is
such a feeling of them having nothing better to do, while their
German neighbours were designing tanks.

The result seems to be that nobody is quite sure where they
stand on Debussy, what they think about him, how far they are
prepared to *love* his music. If that seems on the face of it quite a
preposterous thing to say about one of the world's most loved
great composers, it is not: a very significant quantity of his music
is seldom played and much that is played – the piano music in
particular, and within that the *Préludes* especially – is all too often
played in a hopeful, Impressionistic haze, satisfied with the
sensation of 'isn't it lovely?'

A problem with this – and it underpins the extent to which
that annotation to Jarocinski's book is fair comment – is that the
association of Debussy with Impressionism is so indelible – and
understandably so. Both give us pictures – peculiarly French

pictures, mostly of landscapes, of a nature in which we feel we can see the bobbing quality of light, its rhythm, its *music*. Debussy disliked the comparison, but that does not make the comparison invalid; it was simply that he preferred people to see Debussy as Debussy, not as an inexpensive short-cut to Impressionism. And Debussy as Debussy was alive from 1862 to 1918, a span that gives him more than twenty mature years after the main impact of Impressionism was well spent.

In his *Préludes* for piano he tries to have it both ways, of course; the pieces are given titles, well over half of them explicitly 'landscape' titles, but, significantly, the titles are always printed at the end of a piece, not at the beginning, with three dots in front of them, all in brackets, as if to say that music comes before the guessing game. Interestingly, too, the two 'books' of *Préludes* are in fact not called *Livres*, but *Cahiers*, a word more associated either merely with musical 'exercises' such as a child would have, or an artist's sketchbook, such as Cézanne had.

The loveliness is there – that is not in dispute; as well as the chinoiserie, the wit, the playful imitations, the impression of outdoors. Quite often the loveliness it isn't there, though. Impressionism is a late-nineteenth-century phenomenon and by the time Debussy was writing those pieces, the works of art that were setting the tongues of Paris wagging were the last pictures by Cézanne (around 1906) then the stirrings of Cubism (from 1908). Debussy was, on the one hand, a devoted gallery-goer but, on the other hand, he could be rather disdainful of other people's innovations. His shimmering, outdoor qualities have as much in common with the much earlier works of Antoine Watteau (1684–1721) as with Claude Monet (1840–1926), yet the tetchy, un-Impressionist, firm geometry of Cézanne and the jagged caresses of the Cubists suited his character as much as the rhythmic surges and exuberance of Impressionism. Debussy often alludes to the plucking, prancing whimsy of the mandolin or lute: there are lutes in Watteau, and in every second Cubist portrait by Picasso or Braque, but none in Monet.

Indeed, Debussy had a cruel streak in him, an analytic understanding of himself that he did not like to reveal, a capacity to wound and then to walk away, a sting in his tail. It seems unlikely that he meant to be so with nasty deliberation, it seems more likely that he had so many shy complexes – about his height and his talent and about being in debt or short of money for much of the time, as well as being misunderstood, that his reserve and his knowledge of his true worth required barbed-wire at the perimeter. Within that perimeter he liked his freedom. And the inner freedom within that perimeter gave him an understanding of irony – not to be mistaken for mere sarcasm – that was ever more poignant once Paris itself was besieged in the World War.

He disliked theory. At the Conservatoire he disliked harmony theory and preferred to explore on the keyboard rather than to conform on the page. Later in life, he disliked theory of opera, so fashionable in the wake of Wagner, whose frequently self-contradictory but long-windedly enthusiastic grand theories have little to do with what Wagner at his greatest as a composer then did, and too much to do with what those that followed him did – usually *not* at their greatest. Debussy's attitude to Wagner began with rapt submission, so much so that for his own sake, to preserve his own identity and nurture his own language, he later had to (pretend to) reject him.

Yet throughout his life, Debussy took what he wanted from the music of Wagner and when it came to drama he took what he could work with for his own taste; theory does not really enter into it, but character does. And there the trouble starts, because the slow fate of his opera *Pelléas et Mélisande* (1893–95) – it took five or six long and frustrating years before it was staged – gave the energetic, innovatory, mischievous and direct composer of the *String Quartet* (1892–93) a crisis of nerves that haunted him for the rest of his life. With confidence he called that string quartet his first, but there was never a second. Never again did he have the fluency that he had in the early 1890s.

It is unfair perhaps, but not inaccurate, to put some blame on the opera itself. *Pelléas et Mélisande* is a drama in which the action is languid, the characters all but exhausted and unenthusiastic, and the landscape miserable. For this reason I have placed a simple synopsis of the opera at the centre of this book. It is very nearly all that is needed, to see Debussy's unique vision of something enigmatic and elusive where, in the pessimism of other people, things are respectively meaningless or incomprehensible. All energy is etiolated and Debussy's extraordinary achievement (except for those to whom the opera is simply too boring to be considered) is to see in intricate detail so ravishing a beauty in the smallest mechanism of relentless time – it is so far down in the clock of the world that there is little light, where the cogs are of such thin material that life seems transparent and passion is a fatally destructive but inevitable error.

It was an achievement that may be seen to have cost Debussy his life, for an ecstasy of entropy haunts his character and eventually his health from then on. The success of the opera came slowly, but by the time it came, Debussy felt that it was irrelevant in any case; he did not even attend a performance. His orchestral works thereafter are sumptuous and inasmuch as they are 'tone poems' they are tonally more inventive and poetically more evocative than anyone else's, but that is that. In his piano miniatures, which still confuse most pianists into washes of lovely, lush sound but which, if played with the clarity of Rameau, become nothing less than astonishing, the choice can be summarized between those that are languid and those whose energy is sarcastic or droll. The happy ones tend to be fantastical, about Puck or Mr. Pickwick, but the desolate ones, about dead leaves or wind or snow or fog, are truly, even tragically desolate.

I am not complaining. It is just that we must not expect what is not there – and we should look for what *is* there. For instance, the fact that all of those pieces are prickly often goes for nothing. The prickliness is very subtly achieved but it is there in its wry irony. Take . . . *Brouillards*, the first of the second book of *Préludes*, in which the haze is stabbed in an ominous way; too often it is played with all-purpose sustaining pedal, and the fright – or rather, characteristically with Debussy, the possibility of fright – is overlooked. These are not pretty pictures. If . . . *Des pas sur la neige*, the sixth of the first book, seems 'lovely', it has been badly played; its understanding of forlorn fate is far too disturbing for that.

Or should be. It is for this stabbing sensation of mortality and the exquisite moment of the butterfly nonetheless that Debussy will never leave us. Of all composers before him, Debussy's most unreserved passion and admiration were for Chopin, whose music – however abundantly popular it undoubtedly is – also frequently suffers from underestimation, from performance based merely on prettification of his charms or on superficial emphasis of the drama. Delacroix's description of Chopin's music as an exquisite bird swooping in flight over the horrors of the abyss can as aptly be used of the best of Debussy's music. Indeed, in the three sonatas he wrote during World War One, the joy, the blue of the skies is achieved from exactly that perspective of fright and horror, an all-too-great awareness of the dark abyss into which Europe had collapsed.

This is not 'le twaddle français'; these last sonatas, whatever they cost the composer, enrich music with incalculable strength, a noble inner vision that cannot ultimately be defeated from the outside.

CHAPTER I

THE YOUNG MAN ON HIS WAY

(1862–87)

- ♦ *Early years*
- ♦ *Training at the Conservatoire*
- ♦ *Prizes and failures*
- ♦ *The Prix de Rome*
- ♦ *First compositions*
- ♦ *Return to Paris*

A chille-Claude Debussy was born in St-Germain-en-Laye, in the administrative *département* of Seine-et-Oise, just west of Paris, on 22 August 1862. The town is in the heart of what we think of as Impressionist countryside, with tree-lined leisurely rivers and gentle hills. The birthplace of Louis XIV, St-Germain-en-Laye had a royal pedigree, but despite occasional occurrences of Debussy's family name as 'de Bussy', the composer's family was in fact of humble origin. Even so, the family can be traced back at least as far as the early eighteenth century – at which time, on his father's side, their home country was in Burgundy – and includes among its list of trades those of 'fringe-maker', carpenter and farrier, as well as farmer.

Debussy's parents ran a small china shop at the time of his birth, but within a couple of years they had to move, first to Clichy and then to Paris. His father, Manuel-Achille (1836–1910), eventually found work there, but with some difficulty. The composer used his father's first name, Achille, for many years before changing to his other name, Claude, which came to him from his grandfather. He may have made the change because the name

Achilles, while bringing to mind on the one hand a great Greek hero and warrior, was equally likely, on the other hand, to epitomize vulnerability.

The composer's character was from the outset a mercurial mixture of the definite and the undecided: set in certain ways yet open-minded – heroic but vulnerable. At the piano he was capable of 'forcing all effects', while the music he wrote for piano is, both in terms of colour and effect, the most innovative since Chopin. He tended to deprecate his own talent in comparison with the masters of the past; however, it was a perfectly worthy gesture when, in 1915, he dedicated his twelve piano *Etudes*, or 'Studies', to Chopin.

The young Debussy's natural musical gifts were not quick to establish themselves. Indeed, living in France, which had traditionally always been more excited by painters than by composers, especially in the nineteenth century, it is hardly surprising that his earliest childhood ambitions as a creator were to be a painter, even though his father had harboured the notion that his son might become a sailor. The Paris that the boy found himself growing up in was the Paris of the still-controversial Impressionist painters. From an early age, and throughout his life, he had a good eye, for landscape and weather in particular; it was an eye that grew to be appreciative of the work of the Impressionists just as much as it was essentially nurtured by their vision. We talk of 'having a musical ear', but of Debussy it could be said that he had the finest 'musical eye' of any composer.

At the age of nine, he began piano lessons with an old Italian called Cerutti, who regarded him as nothing out of the ordinary. Gabriel Pierné (1863–1937), one of his friends from this time and later, conductor of some first performances of his music, describes him at about that time as ' . . . fat, short, thickset. . . . His clumsiness and awkwardness were extraordinary, in addition to which he was shy and even unsociable.' If this was the genius that Cerutti not surprisingly failed to spot, one Madame Mauté de Fleurville did not. She had been a pupil of Chopin's and, on hearing Debussy by chance, was immediately struck by echoes of her old master and took him on – at no charge. The rapport between them was extraordinary and within a very short time she put him forward for the entrance examinations for the prestigious Paris Conservatoire.

THE CONSERVATOIRE

Debussy passed the entrance examination and in the autumn of 1893 began his training at the Paris Conservatoire, correctly known as the Conservatoire National Supérieur de Musique, the highest school of music in France, formed in 1795, the year after the Conservatoire National des Arts et Métiers.

He had just turned eleven, and at the Conservatoire found himself, at this impressionable age, at the heart of an élite; the eccentricities and contradictions of his character flourished. Poor as his background was, he had holidayed on the Côte d'Azur with his more wealthy godparents and had glimpsed something of a more exotic and rarified way of life than his circumstances would normally have afforded. He happily allowed his name to appear in its pseudo-aristocratic guise, 'de Bussy', which, with Achille before it, gave his persona an air of sophistication and mystery. Despite his clumsiness, he developed a taste for fine things and – since only on this scale could he begin to think of affording them – for miniature things.

He frequented antique dealers and 'made a clean sweep of tiny Japanese objects which entranced him'. Paris, at this time, was being swept by a fashion for all things oriental – artefacts such as prints, fans and screens as well as laquered furniture were to be seen everywhere. This taste was so sweeping as to be sometimes indiscriminate but it had a specific effect on all the arts. The delicacy of oriental brushwork and the understated quality of oriental paintings were important to the Impressionists in their reaction against the heavily finished and more formal style of painting of the first half of the century. It all found a resonance in Debussy's heart.

As a pianist, his persona was in many ways as unformed, as shy and rough-edged as his general behaviour. Pierné's recollections give a strong flavour of how 'he used to astound us with his bizarre playing':

> Whether it was through natural maladroitness or through shyness I don't know, but he literally used to charge at the piano and force all his effects. He seemed to be in a rage with the instrument, rushing up and down it with impulsive gestures and breathing noisily during the difficult bits. These faults gradually receded and occasionally he would obtain effects of an astonishing softness.

> *With all its faults and virtues, his playing remained something highly individual.*
>
> *He was a gourmet, not a gourmand. He liked nice things and quantity didn't matter to him. I can still remember clearly the way he used to savour the cup of chocolate which my mother would buy him at Prévost's... or the way at Borbonneux's, where there was a window reserved for de luxe items, he would choose a tiny sandwich or a little dish of macaroni, instead of gorging himself on more substantial cakes, like his colleagues. Poor as he was, and from the humblest of origins, he had aristocratic tastes. He showed a particular predilection for miniscule objects and for things that were fragile and delicate.*

Debussy's physical appearance was quite distinctive. Although not tall, he had an imposing head – partly because the large forehead seemed out of proportion. He had a fidgety, shy manner, and walked with short, hurried steps, sometimes behaving as if his appearance in some way embarrassed him.

A fellow student, Raymond Bonheur (1861–1939), gives the following picture of Debussy from those days – having met him in 1878, when he appeared with his mother, wearing short trousers even at the age of sixteen, to be introduced to the new class master:

> *He seemed then to be withdrawn and rather distant, with a marked predilection for everything that was rare and precious, but a singularly attractive person nonetheless, despite a certain brusqueness on first acquaintance; and he was exactly the same when I met him again a few years later on his return from Rome, when he used to enjoy passing the time in the Brasserie Pousset. One noticed his forehead, that powerful forehead with the strange faunlike cast, which he thrust ahead of him like the prow of a ship; his brown eyes, hidden away beneath the frowning eyebrows and obstinately fixed on a point far away directly in front of him, while his index finger in a characteristic gesture tapped the ash from his cigarette.*
>
> *As often happens with people who are not satisfied with clichés and think for themselves, his speech was hesitant and he generally expressed himself in a voice that lisped slightly, in short, incomplete phrases, in monosyllables sometimes, trying his hardest to find a*

word subtle enough to get across the nuance of an impression or a point of view.

With his dark hair, sensual nose and pale face surrounded by a light fringe of beard, Debussy in those days made you think of one of those noble portraits by Titian, and you could easily imagine him in the lavish surroundings of some Venetian palace. Born poor, he entered life with the tastes, needs and carefree attitude of a great lord; nothing upset him more than to be taken for a professional man and the very phrase filled him with a secret horror.

A piece of innocent mystification: at the wedding of one of our friends, for whom we were standing as witnesses, Debussy signed the register in the usual way; then, having to say what his profession was, he thought for a moment before solemnly putting down 'gardener'.

Training at the Conservatoire naturally concentrated on two aspects of music: performance and composition. His sensibility as a composer was brought out in three years of study of harmony with Albert Lavignac (1846–1916), and Debussy was fortunate to strike up an immediately happy rapport with his professor. Lavignac had won first prizes for *solfège* – or harmony – in 1857, for piano in 1861, for harmony and accompaniment in 1863 and for counterpoint and fugue in 1864; he was a complete Conservatoire character, one of whose innovations was the introduction of unseen dictation as part of harmony training.

Lavignac could see Debussy's talent and his individuality and inquisitive sense of invention. Like all young innovators-to-be, Debussy also fancied himself as a rebel against the academic way of doing things and Lavignac's almost unexpected sympathetic admiration of the bizarre extremes of Debussy's genius helped reconcile the young composer, against his instincts, to theory and discipline.

The results of this collaboration between teacher and pupil was a string of successes at the *solfège* examinations: Debussy won third, then second, then first medals in 1874, 1875 and 1876 respectively. Thereafter, his classes were taken by Émile Durand (1830–1903), whose strict academic mind did not suit Debussy's now ever more supple and individual style, let alone his increasing tendency to sloth. Debussy's examination results faltered, but this did not bother him at all. Indeed, quite the opposite, and in later life he was to attack the extremely competitive Conservatoire system as 'absurd' – while also writing competition pieces to be played as set pieces in the examinations!

Durand was, in essence, a hack who had had early slight success and then quickly settled into a teaching career of eternal repetition of rigid exercises. He wrote a few light operas. All the same, contemporaries report that Debussy's wild and unconventional exercises brought from his teacher an increasing admiration and fascination, despite himself. Perhaps his strictness even helped prompt Debussy into teasing flashes of forbidden chromatics, but at any rate his ears pricked up – even if he continued to mark Debussy down. And he was to be rewarded with the dedication of Debussy's charming *Piano Trio* of 1880.

THE YOUNG PIANIST

Meanwhile, Debussy was less lucky at the piano. His first teacher at the Conservatoire was Antoine-François Marmontel (1816–98), then in his late fifties. He had won the piano prize in 1832 and had gone on to teach a good number of France's most distinguished pianists and composers, including Georges Bizet (1838–75), Isaac Albéniz (1860–1909) and Vincent d'Indy (1851–1931), as well as Debussy's composition teacher Ernest Guiraud (1837–92) and Francis Planté (1839–1934), a strange character who suddenly retired from the concert platform and 'from public view' around 1900 but made a come-back fifteen years later, keeping his vow by playing from behind a screen – including some music by Debussy.

Marmontel went on teaching until just short of his seventieth birthday, writing the usual clutch of manuals and exercises, as well as a history of the piano. Predictably, his strict and unimaginative discipline did little to inspire the wayward young student with the eccentrically compelling style. Like Durand, however, Marmontel could see Debussy's natural talent – and, also like Durand, he could not see how to accommodate it within the scheme of things at the Conservatoire. He once commented that Debussy 'is not fond of the piano but he is very fond of music', an odd combination of insight and error. He was, at any rate, celebrating the composer's natural and fluent gift while lamenting nothing more than his extreme reluctance ever to practise, let alone to work on exercises, and in his way Debussy became rather fond of this caring adversary. In fact, Marmontel did encourage his more wayward pupils, but more by haphazard encouragement than by insight or guile.

At that time, Debussy showed a taste for the work of a number of composers, spanning a long period and a wide musical spectrum: J.S. Bach (1685–1750), Mozart (1756–91), Chopin (1810–49) and Schumann (1810–1856) most of all, as well as Haydn (1732–1809) and Alkan (1813–88). He liked the music of Weber (1786–1826), but tended to detest Beethoven (1770–1827). He liked openness, and with Beethoven (and to a certain extent with Wagner) he had an edgy fear of the composer's manner of certainty, of what could be called his 'closing the book' or 'banging the table'. With Wagner he had a positively love-hate relationship; with Beethoven, there was none of the love.

These composers whom he most adored are notable for two characteristics. Firstly, there is with Bach and Chopin, Mozart and Haydn, a sprightly combination of dance and clarity that underpins their music and which is also an important element in the muse that inspired Debussy's best music, and not merely his piano music. In the case of Schumann and Charles-Valentin Alkan however, the respectively wayward and extreme technical demands at the keyboard serve a poetic purpose often by setting out to make a pictorial effect, or to render wordlessly the mood or drama of a character or text. Their music is seldom abstract as it is with the more classical composers. This, too, is an important feature of Debussy's music. We can also see here the origins of the two overall styles of playing Debussy's piano works – styles that veer from extremes of sharp clarity to the most densely wistful haze. The composer's own taste was always for clarity of texture above all.

His parents hoped that their son would prove to be a virtuoso – now that a career as a sailor seemed doomed. With hindsight it is easy to see that his unconventional and inventive character was really positioning itself as a composer, rather than as a performer, but Debussy had some ambitions at the keyboard too. Already, when he was a month short of his twelfth birthday, he received 'Second Honourable Mention' in the Advanced Piano Competition, for his account of Chopin's *Piano Concerto No.2 in F minor*. This was not merely an internal 'school' event, but one reported on even in the newspapers. After all, France may have lost the Franco-Prussian war a couple of years before, but that merely served to redouble its pride in its traditions of competitive artistic sovereignty.

A year later, in 1875, Debussy achieved 'First Honourable Mention' for his way with the set piece, on this occasion Chopin's *Ballade No.2*. The year before, critics had attributed his prize to his being so young that errors could be forgiven; this time they hailed him as a prodigy and a promising virtuoso in his own right.

In 1876, however, that lull after success had set in – always the rhythm of his life – and he was not even mentioned in the newspapers. The set piece had been the first movement of Beethoven's *Piano Sonata* Op.111, his last, the melodramatic rage of which did not suit the boy in the least. Or, perhaps it did, in a paradoxical way: Marmontel's class was in general picked out for mannerisms, affectation and exhibitionism, all of which must have been at the heart of Debussy's probably ironic, possibly pastiching version of the movement. Debussy was always in his element verbally, when called upon for a barbed comment, so why not also at the keyboard? What he would have done with the sonata's dreamy and ecstatic second movement, on the other hand, can only be conjecture.

A review of a concert given in January 1876 gives evidence of how the thirteen-and-a-half-year-old de Bussy [sic] was progressing, carrying, as the reviewer says, 'so much courage inside such a small body. What verve! What enthusiasm! What real spirit! Never again can it be said that the piano is a cold instrument, that the finger which strikes the key is such a long way from the string that vibrates, that its life is lost along the way or that the sound is dead!'

And so it went on. In the following year, 1877, the set piece was the first movement of Schumann's *Piano Sonata* Op.22, a movement of frantic, restless energy in which at one point the tempo marking 'as fast as possible' is followed by 'faster' and then by 'even faster'. Debussy took second prize, sharing it with Camille Bellaigue (1858–1930). This fellow student became a music critic for the influential *Revue des Deux Mondes*, and took a significantly anti-Debussy stance. He published the following reminiscence of the 'frequently late, small, sickly-looking' Debussy at the Conservatoire:

His blouse was held in by a belt and he carried in his hand a sort of beret with braid around the outside and a woollen pompom in the middle, like the hats that sailors wear. Nothing about the young Debussy, neither his looks nor his comments, nor his playing, suggested an artist, present or future. His face had nothing striking about it except his forehead . . . I particularly remember his idiosyncracy, or rather a tic, of emphasizing the strong beats in the bar with a sort of hiccup or raucous gasp. This exaggeration of the rhythms was later to be the least of his faults, in the field of composition at least, if not perhaps in his piano playing. He was very withdrawn, not to say surly, and was not regarded sympathetically by his fellow students.

There was always the pressure of honour (if not always of actual musicianship) for winners of the second prize in one year to go on to win first prize the next year. It was expected – to the extent that the status of winning a second prize was greatly diminished by a failure to take first prize the following year. Bellaigue did exactly that in 1878, taking first prize with a movement from a sonata by Weber. Debussy received no prize, although some of the reviews made it plain that he had their sympathy. That was hardly enough and he was, not unnaturally, despondent at the outcome. He had not cured his lazy attitude – if anything it then deepened. In the competition a year later, the critic of *La Revue et Gazette Musicale* said that he seemed 'to be progressing backwards'. That was in 1879, when the test piece was from his beloved Chopin again.

Just at this moment, with poor showings in harmony as well as in his playing, Debussy's life took a special turn that lifted him out of all despondency. Through the good offices of Marmontel, he was recommended as pianist to the household of Nadezhda von Meck, a post that he held for three consecutive summers, between 1880 and 1882.

TRAVELS IN STYLE
Born in 1831, Mme. von Meck had been the wife of a Russian railway contractor, widowed in her mid-forties. She used her wealth to creative purpose, most famously giving Tchaikovsky (1840–1893) a generous allowance, at any rate until 1890, when it ended because of her not surprising financial difficulties. Even

when having him entertained on her estate, however, she never met him. It is said that they once passed in the street; yet they kept up a fascinating and revealing correspondence. She lived a life of wealthy leisure, going from resort to resort and from home to home according to the season. For the summer of 1880, when Debussy was employed as her pianist, she wrote to Tchaikovsky that he had been taken on 'to give lessons to the children, to accompany [her daughter] Julia's singing and to play piano duets with me. The young man plays well, his technique is brilliant, but he's lacking in sensibility. He is still too young. He says he's twenty, but looks sixteen.'

In fact, he was within a month of his eighteenth birthday. Soon after, Mme. von Meck wrote to Tchaikovsky of Debussy's uncanny skill at sight-reading, at his way of reading a score, 'even one of yours, like a book', and of his admiration of Tchaikovsky's music. Later evidence suggests that this may have been an expression more of tact than sincerity. He did however profess, with all honesty, a disinterest in German music – 'heavy and unclear' – and overall he left her with an impression of 'a typical product of the Parisian boulevards. He composes very nicely as well, but in that, too, he's a perfect Frenchman.'

His early compositions from these years have not all survived. Most substantial is the recently discovered yet still seldom heard *Piano Trio in G major*, dedicated to his teacher Durand and completed in Fiesole, just north of Florence, in the summer of 1880, while on tour with the von Meck household. If it did not have quite so light a French touch, the opening theme's way of turning in on itself would seem almost Brahmsian; and the second movement is a particularly breezy *scherzo*, a charming piece of chinoiserie, itself in this repertoire quite a novelty.

It is an interesting detail that the composer marked the score as the 'First Trio', even though a second trio was never written nor have any sketches survived; he did the same with his *String Quartet*. It is as if Debussy were playing a part, and perhaps the extraordinary atmosphere of the von Meck household, unreal enough even in those days, brought out this side of him.

Yet role-playing was an aspect of his self-doubt that was plainly visible throughout his life, expressed sometimes by sheer astonishment and humble exhaustion when he had indeed completed a big piece.

Perhaps it was part of his awkwardness or perhaps part of the 'airs' he gave himself in the von Meck household that prompted the affectation or arrogance of calling the trio his 'first'. He still liked to use the 'de Bussy' form of his name too – an exercise in vanity, which a friend nonetheless later said 'could not have lasted with someone of his mocking habits'. At any rate, his employer was, in general, happy with the musician she called 'her little Frenchman', keeping him on a few weeks longer than contracted and, indeed, releasing him only on the refusal of the Conservatoire to grant him leave of absence. When the day of departure came, he wept bitterly. Clearly, he had felt at home among the well-to-do, the cultured aristocracy. He also liked to be somewhere where he was appreciated.

Mme. von Meck's son Nicholas adds to the picture a memoir that is a shade formal, as he strives to be 'correct' – about a man who, for his part, certainly never strove to be anything of the kind:

> *The little Frenchman arrived, dark, thin, sarcastic, and gave everybody amusing nicknames. . . . He joined us in Switzerland, and from there we went to Italy and stopped in Rome. Once we walked past the Villa Medici, where the best students of the Conservatoire reside for a year at the cost of the French government. One of us, pointing to the villa, said to Debussy: 'This is your future home.' It was interesting to see how longingly he looked back on the Villa Medici.*
>
> *From Rome we went to Florence, where we lived at the Villa Oppenheim, and from there, in October, Debussy returned to his studies in Paris. On leaving us he was very sad, and my mother had to comfort him, promising him that in the spring he would again return to us. . . . My mother considered Debussy a gifted musician, not only as a pianist but also as a composer. He was a pupil of Massenet [this is inaccurate but perhaps it stems from Debussy's self-puff at the time], and at that time his professor exercised a strong influence on him.*
>
> *My mother acquainted him with Russian music and with Wagner. Of the Russians he got to know Tchaikovsky and all the members of the Kutchka* [the Mighty Handful], *Rimsky-Korsakov, Cui, Mussorgsky and Borodin.*
>
> *Both Wagner and the Russian composers produced an unfavourable impression on Debussy, which was quite natural,*

> *since French music at that time was too near the music of the classical composers, and Debussy, following this tradition, did not react to all innovations.*
>
> *But as he became better acquainted with Russian music he appreciated it, though by his French nature he was inclined to interpret it in a superficial and elegant manner. No doubt his acquaintance not only with Russian music and Wagner, but also with his contemporaries in other countries, widened his outlook and influenced his development.*
>
> *Of his compositions at that time his song* 'Içi-bas tous les lilas meurent' *('There where all the lilac dies') was frequently sung and played in my house by my sister.*

The Russian influence on Debussy is important, although its extent has been exaggerated. Indeed, Debussy was later accused of particular 'debt' to Modest Mussorgsky (1839–81), yet he was able to point out that although the von Meck library contained many of his scores, they were unplayed; Mussorgsky's music was fairly unknown even in those circles. His debt to Mussorgsky's great opera *Boris Godunov* is nothing like the debt he owed – and suppressed – to Wagner's *Parsifal*. Raymond Bonheur recalled that even from his trip to Russia with the von Meck household, Debussy brought back only the score of an old opera by Rimsky-Korsakov and some Borodin songs; 'It was not until around 1893 at Luzancy, where Chausson was kind enough to offer us his hospitality, that Mussorgsky was revealed to us. We were burning to get to know *Boris Godunov*, but it was then almost impossible to get hold of a score. Chausson, however, managed to do so and for hours at a time, over entire evenings, Debussy would be at the piano, initiating us into this amazing work.'

At any rate, his contact with Russian music was strengthened by the fact that the following year he had to travel to Russia, to meet the von Meck household for the second summer of his employment. He found Tchaikovsky's music less satisfactory than the music of his more raw Russian compatriots. Later he told the writer and composer Cyril Scott (1879–1970) that he disliked Tchaikovsky 'ardently' and that he deplored the 'British taste which could set up such a vulgarian as an idol to be worshipped', while overlooking the true Russian composers such as Rimsky-Korsakov and Mussorgsky. At that time, early in the twentieth century, the British taste was so beguiled by the symphonies of Brahms, Dvořák and Tchaikovsky for his newly-founded Promenade Concerts, Sir Henry Wood had been asked by his directors to play the Tchaikovsky *Symphony No.6*, the *'Pathétique'*, every single night!

Despite Nicholas von Meck's observations about French characteristics, the influence of the Russians had a direct bearing on the French temperament in a way that German music did not. The Russian style of orchestration was much more French in that it looked back to Berlioz rather than across to Wagner. It was marked by a particular translucency, gained by a balance towards the woodwind and the higher range of instruments than was the German model. Because of this, it seemed to be lighter on its feet as well as more outdoor in mood; colours seemed more fleeting or ephemeral, like leaves in a wind, than in the more solidly etched contours of German and Viennese music.

It is interesting to note that Debussy's life was framed by two major defeats for France. In July 1870, France had declared war on Prussia and had quickly lost; Paris had been beseiged for four months, before falling in January 1871. By the treaty that followed, France lost Alsace and Lorraine and had to pay a large indemnity – five billion francs. Equally, there had always been a happier relationship between France and Russia; twenty years later, the decade of the 1890s was marked by a sequence of more or less formal treaties and agreements with Russia to act together should either be attacked by Germany, Italy or Austro-Hungary. In the spring of 1918, towards the end of World War One, Debussy was not to live to see the Germans pushed back into Belgium, and his entire experience of the war was one of defeat, hopelessness and gloom.

The young composer was by now setting his sights on the Prix de Rome, and his personal musical tastes, allegiances and sympathies were more important than those of the political world; it was necessary that he define these for himself along with his likes and dislikes – even if these were based on superficial or intuitive responses. The Russian palette in particular was attractive to him, and one or two songs that he composed at this time show influences from Borodin; he was also intrigued by the Russian skill at conjuring up, with the ease of an artist, scenes that were strange and exotic.

For the competition there was also the need to show a certainty of touch that, as a composer, he never found entirely easy or natural, however immediate the results sound.

THE YOUNG COMPOSER AND THE PRIX DE ROME

The Conservatoire had reorganized certain classes and Debussy joined the new classes in Piano Accompaniment. The professor was one Auguste Bazille (1828–91), director of singing at the Opéra-Comique and winner of a second prize in the 1848 Prix de Rome. The importance to Debussy of these classes was great, for they helped develop his already natural instincts not only to improvize but also to conjure orchestral sound from the keyboard. They thus provided a marvellous match for his pianism and his early compositional skills all in one. An account by his classmate Maurice Emmanuel (1862–1938) captures the happy mood of rebellion and instruction that these classes inspired:

> *Debussy, who felt at his ease with the conscientious and broad-minded Bazille, soon reached the stage when he could extemporize at the piano harmonic exercises that were well-balanced and finished in style. He was fond of adding interesting passing-notes to his basses; he endeavoured to break the monotony of harmonic sequences, whose recurrence was inevitable, by varying the melodic contour of the upper parts – a proceeding which at first scandalized Bazille, who however soon gave way. . . . Bazille did not always approve of the underlying modulations in which his pupil indulged. But, just as Marmontel had realized the spontaneity of Debussy's talent in spite of his carelessness and eccentricity, so Bazille also, listened, growled, stormed, but ultimately gave in.*

Inspired by a year of such classes, Debussy could sense his career as a composer was about to take root. A path seemed to become clearer to him. He was also about to fall in love.

Partly to earn money as well as to gain experience, he had taken up work as accompanist at the singing classes held by Mme. Moreau-Sainti; there he met the young and elegant, attractive wife of a Parisian architect called Vasnier and became a frequent guest at their house. Indeed, Debussy worked with them both in Paris and in a small villa they rented for the summers at Ville-d'Avray, a leisurely suburb just west of Paris, near Nanterre, and associated with the painter Corot. He had asked if he could live and work with them because of the lack of understanding and support of his own family – at any rate, that was the not-strictly-exact excuse that he gave. He found himself in a considerably more comfortable as well as more cultured setting for four or five years. And he fell in love with Mme. Vasnier; their affair lasted until about 1890.

The family were immediately fond of him. Indeed, their daughter, Marguerite (1869–1935) wrote a memoir of Debussy, published in the 1 May 1926 issue of *La Revue Musicale*. At their summer villa, Debussy would come by the first train and return by the last, sometimes dependent on winning at cards in the evening to be able to afford his fare for the day. If he lost at cards he would be furious, but they would then slip a packet of tobacco into his napkin at dinner. We are fortunate to have the following account, written by Marguerite in 1926, for his own family would never have been likely to leave so distinctly-observed a portrait.

> *At eighteen Debussy was a large, beardless boy, with clearly defined features and thick, black, curly hair which he wore plastered down over his forehead. But when, at the end of the day, his hair became unruly (which suited him much better) he was, my parents said, the image of a Florentine from the Middle Ages. It was a very interesting face; the eyes, especially, attracted your attention; you felt that here was a personality. His hands were strong and bony, with square fingers; his touch on the piano was sonorous, rather percussive but also sometimes very gentle and* cantabile. . . .
>
> *He used to work long hours, but sometimes we went for long walks in the park of Saint-Cloud or played interminable games of croquet. He was very good at it, but a bad loser. Out in the countryside he would sometimes become as carefree and cheerful as a child. For our walks in the woods, he refused to wear a straw hat, preferring a large, blue felt one which he wore to one side; one day, as the eternal cigarette had singed the rim slightly, someone covered up the hole by sewing a piece of blue velvet over it, and this sent him into ecstasies. Sometimes he would turn his stick into a guitar and pretend to be a Florentine singer, improvising ditties and serenades or parodying Italian music, which he didn't care for. . . . He had moments of extreme gaiety like that, but these*

would be followed by hours of gloom and discouragement....

He had his own decided tastes in everything; he was very fond of blue and used to be very careful choosing the colours of everything he wore.... He was moody, touchy and sensitive in the highest degree: the slightest thing could cheer him up, but could likewise send him into a rage. He was unsociable, and did not disguise his discontent when my parents entertained, because he usually refused to meet strangers and this meant he could not come to the house. If by chance he did meet them, and they were lucky enough to find favour in his eyes, he could be charming, playing and singing Wagner, imitating and caricaturing some modern composer; but when they did not find favour, he knew how to register the fact. He was an original and slightly unpolished individual, but utterly charming with those he liked.

Being extremely ignorant and too intelligent to be unaware of it, he used to read voraciously during the long summer days when he couldn't compose or go for a walk, and I often found him hunting among my schoolbooks for the dictionary, which he studied conscientiously. 'I'm very fond of reading the dictionary,' he used to say: 'you learn any number of interesting things from it.' He had an innate taste in judging any kind of art, even for pictures and engravings, which, in those days at least, did not interest him at all. When my father, who was a great lover of painting, got Debussy talking on the subject, he found his judgement sure and his opinions completely personal and quite remarkable.

It was Marguerite's father, too who more than anyone pushed Debussy to give him the momentum required to make a good showing in the Prix de Rome competition. Although Debussy scorned the ethos of competition that existed at the Conservatoire, he was not so unrealistic as to think that he could progress without such successes. His relative lack of success after a good start bothered him. Scorn for competition always registers better when voiced by a winner, of course, and it was quite natural therefore that as a composer he should set his sights on the Prix de Rome.

The Prix de Rome was a prize awarded by the Académie des Beaux-Arts, itself part of the Institut de France. There could be no higher award. The 'members' of the French academies, who were elected for life and known as the *Immortels*, had an institutionalized authority in French life like no other. The Institut is made up of five 'academies': the Académie Française, originally established by Richelieu in 1635; the Académie des Inscriptions et Belles-lettres; the Académie des Sciences – these dating from the time of the Enlightenment, in the 1660s; then the Académie des Beaux-Arts and the Académie des Sciences Morales et Politiques, which date from 1795. Especially in the context of the way Wagner's music had seized the imagination – and anger – of Europe, the prize had become even more nationalistic than before; French music could parade its armies against the Germanic tide, where the country's actual armies had suffered defeat so recently.

Debussy's attitude to the prize was, as ever, ambivalent. He saw its necessity in his career but in the end he did little to curtail his style or imagination in order to be more certain of winning over the jury. The prize awarded each year in each of the arts was a two-year sojourn in Rome, at the Villa Medici, with all expenses paid. The winners were expected to send back to Paris the fruits of their studies and industry, pieces known as their *envois*. Debussy had little desire to go to Rome and consequently his attempt was only half-hearted. He loved Paris and had found a repertoire of friends with whom he could escape the strictures of his own home, not to mention Mme. Vasnier. Rome would be a bore – to be cooped up with fellow students, not merely musicians but the painters and others as well.

Yet he worked for it. He also had to submit to the ritual whereby candidates were shut up in the Conservatoire to write their submissions – literally confined to 'hermetically-sealed studios' for more than three weeks. Visitors were allowed at certain times, and Debussy's parents and the Vasniers, too, would appear, in order to keep his spirits up. Marguerite Vasnier's reminiscences also give an amusing account of Debussy at work as a composer, both in their home and incarcerated in the Conservatoire:

> *He used to arrive most evenings and often in the afternoon as well, leaving the manuscript paper on a little table until later. He composed at the piano, a curiously shaped old Blondel. At other times, he would compose walking about. He used to improvise at length, then walk up and down the room singing to*

himself, with his eternal cigarette in his mouth or rolling paper and tobacco in his fingers. Then, when he'd found the idea, he wrote it down. He never crossed out a great deal, but he searched a long time in his head before writing anything down and was highly critical of his own work. . . .

He was preparing to go in for the Prix de Rome. His heart was not in it; I don't know whether, but for my father, he would have refused to try, but I'm certain he would have resigned afterwards and that he was only prevented from doing so by the fear of incurring my father's displeasure. He went in for the prize twice, the first time with Le Gladiateur. *He only came second and certainly relief at staying in Paris more than compensated for any disappointment – the very idea of being shut up for weeks on end filled him with horror. We would often go and see him while he was immured in the Conservatoire for the prize. The contenders received their parents and friends in a courtyard in the garden, where we stayed as long as possible in order to comfort him. He pointed to the window of his room and, when I asked him why there were bars across it, replied: 'No doubt because they think we're wild beasts.'*

The second time, he won the prize. But when, some months later, he had to leave for Rome, he was in despair and wrote letters of bitter desolation.

The ritual of incarcerated composition, ludicrous as it now seems, was matched by a complexity of procedure for judgement that seems just as splendidly ludicrous. There were three prizes on offer, the First Grand Prix de Rome and two Second Grands Prix. The composition had to be a cantata. The initial voting was by members of the music section of the Académie, in a complicated system of successive ballots, interspersed by discussion, which continued until a candidate had achieved five votes. Thereafter, the second session consisted of voting by the entire Académie française.

In 1883, Paul Vidal (1863–1931) won the the first ballot of the first session, with six votes, while one Charles René and Debussy received four and three respectively. Debussy eventually beat René on the fourth ballot of the first session. In the second session Vidal won – with twenty-five votes out of a possible thirty-two – and after no fewer than four rounds of further balloting Debussy eventually secured twenty votes and thus the second prize.

His disappointment, such as it was, was diminished by the manner in which the Press received his cantata, *Le Gladiateur*. Their praise plucked the strings of his vanity and actually provided him with a spur to try to take first prize the following year. This he did, with his cantata *L' Enfant prodigue*. In June 1884, this time on only the second ballot, Debussy achieved the five votes needed in the first session and in the second full session, this time with a possible maximum of twenty-eight votes, he scored twenty-two and took the First Grand Prix.

It is curiously apt, given that Debussy has become thought of – rightly or wrongly – as *the* composer of French Impressionism, that his success in 1884 was reputed to be thanks most of all to the vote of the painters of the *Académie*.

Debussy could now look his parents squarely in the face – he was not quite a 'prodigal son', but was nevertheless a son who, as a composer, had now realized the highest ambitions for him that they could ever hold.

RELUCTANTLY TO ROME

In January 1885, as late as possible within the rules of the prize, Debussy set off for Rome, a 'city of marble and fleas' as he called it. Some of his Paris ways went with him. He continued to collect butterflies and little curios, ivory miniatures in particular. But neither Rome, the ancient capital, nor Italy, home of the Renaissance, interested him greatly.

The contrast between Rome and Paris gives a good commentary on conflicting aspects of his character. Rome was solid and ancient, the Villa Medici was beautiful and Debussy's stay there was the tangible reward of an honourable prize. Worthiness inspired in Debussy a mixture of rebellion and discomfort, even resentment. Paris was, on the other hand, at one and the same time, the capital of a proud but defeated nation as well as the centre of a new European sense of ease and expansion – the prototype of a new style of city, opened up by wide boulevards, busy with buses and alive to the momentum of mass-production and new technology.

Paris suited Debussy's forward-looking energy just as France's mood of shrugging off defeat suited his complexes about his looks, his background and his achievements, none of them as glowing as he would have liked. Rome helped him to focus on this. On M. Vasnier's advice, for instance, he now dropped the pseudo-aristocratic form of his name. Unhappy with his friends in the Villa Medici, he was on the other hand clearly becoming much more aware of what made him happy within himself.

The painter Gustave Popelin (1859–1937) became one of his friends at the Villa, and Debussy confessed to him how much he missed Mme. Vasnier. Indeed, he was 'madly' in love with her, and confinement at the Villa was making his yearning intolerable. All this was made worse by the fact that her husband had become the composer's best mentor, encouraging his self-confidence as well as disciplining him from his excesses. Through a friend of Popelin's, Debussy secured the offer of the use that summer of a house at Fiumicino, by the sea – escape! – and wrote afterwards to M. Vasnier:

> *Ah! I could satisfy my unsociable instincts as much as I wanted, not knowing anyone, talking only to order food (which certainly gave me a lot of trouble). I worked almost well; I took walks, as if I had done so since I was born. Perhaps my seaside was as good as yours, come on!*

It is not unfair to say that much of Debussy's moaning about Rome seems to have been a tone he enjoyed to adopt. He certainly made no effort to feel otherwise and his fellow students evidently found his attitude as painful as he did them. Of the Debussy of the previous years (1880–84), one of his biographers could only sigh and say that he 'really must have been most annoying and exasperating'; of the Rome years, this is actually documented. Some go so far as to say that his unhappiness was 'much exaggerated' or that his long lamentations should be read 'with some skepticism' as the wailing of a 'child-martyr'. True, one benefit to come from his extremely antisocial nature was that he read a great deal, and widely, but the fact remains that his actual composition of music was only fitful.

Indeed, his time in Rome became fitful in every aspect. Despite his ardent love for Mme. Vasnier, he had an affair with one Mme. Hochon and in his second year (1886) managed to secure a two-month leave to return to Paris – partly to see *both* women. He abandoned more projects in Rome than he completed and by far the most substantial piece to come of the stay was the orchestral poem *Printemps*; Debussy remained in Rome a couple of months over his required time in order to finish it in February 1887. Indirectly inspired by Botticelli's painting *Prima-vera* (in Florence), it was presented to the Conservatoire as his final *envoi*, in a two-piano version that did not impress his masters.

Then, in 1887, despite inevitable difficulties over money at this stage, he finally returned to Paris independent, needing – and increasingly able – to map out his future for himself. He was home at last.

CHAPTER 2
YEARS OF DEDICATION
(1888–1900)

- ♦ *Taste in poetry*
- ♦ *Taste – and distaste – for Wagner*
- ♦ *The friends – and women – in his life*
- ♦ *The String Quartet*
- ♦ *The Prélude à 'L' Après-midi d'un faune'*

Most of the projects that Debussy abandoned in the 1880s were operatic, or at any rate dramatic. They included a working of Flaubert's novel *Salammbô* and even of Shakespeare's *As You Like It*, clearly a favourite text of Debussy's – there are at least three abandoned plans for either an operatic treatment or for incidental music. His only writing for piano during this time was either for songs or arrangements of music by other composers. The arrangements were a useful source of income; as late as 1889 the publisher Jacques Durand issued his two-piano arrangement of Saint-Saëns's *Introduction et Rondo capriccioso*, for instance. Arrangements also helped to keep Debussy's name in the publisher's mind. Durand was the second generation of the Durand family to run the firm that was to become by far the most important in the composer's life.

Even as early as this it seems as if Debussy found inspiration as a composer most easily – and looked for it most hopefully – in external sources; not in music but in literature or in painting, even in 'views' themselves, in the sights and smells of nature, in the seasons more than in the sounds. He wrote songs throughout his life, almost exclusively to French texts, although there are a couple of settings of Heine in translation. Song satisfied both his need of an external support to the inner workings of the music as well as his concern to produce something both entirely self-sufficient and 'miniature'. In Rome he had begun a sequence of six *Ariettes*, which were published in 1888; by the time he left, he had written one and sketched two. However, until *Pelléas et Mélisande* was out of the way, the bulk of his attention was on orchestral and vocal music.

The first important such piece is *La Damoiselle élue*, sketched in Rome and completed eventually in Paris, in 1888. The poem is by Dante Gabriel Rossetti (1828–82), although it is interesting that Debussy set words that differ from – and improve the accuracy of – the then published translation. Rossetti was the leading poet of the Pre-Raphaelite movement, which set out, in the increasingly brutal, urban, industrialized and 'realistic' Victorian age, to return to the wispy, dreamy and ethereal values not quite accurately associated with art before and including Raphael (1483–1520).

The movement had enormous impact on French literature. For one thing, poets addicted to the dreamy effect followed a direction that led to a movement known as Symbolism, whose first steps were taken by Charles Baudelaire (1821–67), followed by Lautréamont (1846–70), Verlaine (1844–96), Rimbaud (1854–91) and Mallarmé (1842–98). At the same time, an exotic, sometimes almost cruel offshoot of Symbolism arose, its origins more in the grotesque of Edgar Allan Poe (1809–49) than the dreamy world of Rossetti; Poe had first been translated into French by Baudelaire and these translations influenced Lautréamont in particular, inspiring a movement called the Decadents – a movement that included the ultrarealist writer J.K. Huysmans (1848–1907). In his behaviour, which was sometimes self-conscious and 'posey', Debussy was capable of expressing some sympathy with the Decadents, and indeed, the only two opera settings he made any progress with, other than *Pelléas*, were works by Poe.

His sympathies were far more with Verlaine and Mallarmé. Verlaine in particular was striving for poetic effects that were achieved in sound rather than merely through the meaning of the words. An example can be found in *Clair de lune*, the poem whose title Debussy took for his best known piano piece. This poem comes from a collection called *Fêtes galantes* (1869), poems that revel in the courtly and colourful decadence of the outdoor night-parties in the fanciful gardens painted by Watteau. The landscapes there always include almost lewd statuary enacting the passions that the figures themselves merely skirt in their silk breeches and lavish dresses. There is usually a man with a phallic lute or mandolin and the sun sinking behind an erotic tangle of trees. Sometimes these are masked parties and in this poem Verlaine allies the word *masques* with *bergamasques*; the latter word meaning 'from Bergamo' and sometimes used to designate old Italian dance tunes – the perfect assonance and *jeu de mots* for the scene.

The entire Symbolist movement was determined to write about the life behind appearances, the inner workings and magic of things, in an era in which the superficial and material – and the serious – were in their stride. In his manifesto poem *Art poétique* (1875), appealing to music throughout the nine verses, Verlaine insists that words be chosen with a certain carelessness; 'nuance' is the key, the only force that can 'marry dream with dream, the flute to the horn'. The last line says simply: 'All the rest is just literature.' Ironically, it can be said that it was the essential mission of the Impressionists too, to resist the solidity of mid-nineteenth-century painting; only their method of dismissing that heavily obsessive surface 'accuracy' was to exalt the shimmer of appearances. Debussy works in both ways.

Indeed, Debussy also set many poems by Leconte de Lisle (1818–94) and Théodor de Banville (1823–91), slightly older writers whose allegiance was more to the antique than to these dreamy theories, but whose careers spanned into and helped nurture the later groups or movements. Along with Théophile Gautier (1811–72) and promoted by the critical writings of Catulle Mendès (1841–1909), this group was known as the Parnassians, writers devoted to idealized beauty and perfection of expression, still writing in something of a grand style, in tall columns of long lines. Symbolist poems, by contrast, tended to be short, mercurial and with free, carefully spontaneous versification – descriptive terms that will do equally well for all Debussy's greatest piano pieces – the *Préludes*, *Estampes* and *Images* for example. It is not difficult to see that although such ideals are hardly the poetical equivalent of a steam engine, they nonetheless have more in common with the heavily serious Victorian tone than with the flighty, allusive touch of the Symbolists reacting against that austerity. Their attractiveness to Debussy was possibly less in their actual poetic relationship with his music than in the clear light of their 'antique' vision.

Attempts to link Debussy's aesthetic with one movement more than another are skewed by the fact that he lived at a time when French poetry was both abundant and extremely diverse; he took what he wanted. And what he had to have, above all else, was a precision and a wistful quality. Evocation was more important than description, and all the groups, however much at odds with one another in theory, were reacting against the railway age in their different ways. If there is a problem with these various schools and groups, it is that they can seem arch and self-consciously arty as well as melancholy; in this context it is significant that it was the Impressionists who were capable of the detachment that comes with irony. This is especially true of Monet – most of all in his sequence of magically real pictures of the smokey din and joyful anticipation . . . of railway stations!

CONSOLIDATION

The 1880s saw Debussy mark out his ground. By 1889 he had finished *La Damoiselle élue*, although his stubbornness with the Conservatoire meant that the performance of it, to which he was entitled on his return from Rome, was cancelled. Also completed were the set of six *Ariettes* (with texts by Verlaine) and a set of *Cinq Poèmes de Charles Baudelaire* as well as the two *Arabesques* for piano and the *Petite Suite* for piano duet. He was not making a quick start – some of his fellows were published sooner or performed more often than he – but, despite the number of abandoned projects, it was a well varied start of good quality, for all of these pieces have remained in the repertoire.

One curiosity to have survived from these years gives us rather more information about Debussy at the close of the 1880s than might be expected. It is a questionnaire he completed in February 1889, but which was published only in 1903, in a magazine. The questions in the original were in English; these are some of Debussy's answers:

Your favourite virtue?	Pride.
Your favourite quality in men?	Will.
Your favourite quality in women?	Charm.
Your favourite occupation?	Reading while smoking rare tobacco mixtures.

Your chief characteristic?	My hair.
Your idea of happiness?	To love.
Your idea of misery?	To be too hot.
Your favourite colour?	Violet.
If not yourself, who would you be?	A sailor.
Where would you like to live?	Anywhere beyond the world.
Your favourite prose authors?	Flaubert and Edgard Poè. [sic]
Your favourite poets?	Baudelaire.
Your favourite painters and composers?	Botticelli, Gustave Moreau, Palestrina, Bach, Wagner. [yes!]
Your favourite heroes in fiction?	Hamlet.
Your favourite heroines in fiction?	Rosalind. [*As You Like It*]
Your favourite food and drink?	Russian food, coffee.
Your pet aversion?	Dilettantes, women who are too pretty.
For what fault have you the most toleration?	Errors in harmony.
Your favourite motto?	'Always Toward Higher Things.'

Today, we are used to such exercises in the Sunday newspapers, but this must have been the first time a great composer found himself so schematically interviewed. To the question, 'What is your present state of mind?', he replied for the day itself: 'Sad, a seeker, but not on 15 February 1889.'

The transition to the 1890s was one of severe challenges. In his personal life it was signalled by the end of his relationship with Mme. Vasnier. This affair had become increasingly difficult; he was indebted to her husband for support and advice, and as the liaison became increasingly evident, it taxed both men to keep gossip at bay. The story was everything we would expect of the French of the *bel époque*. They had to correspond through an intermediary and their meetings were sometimes risky appointments: in Dieppe in 1887, a painter friend caught sight of Debussy, late one shadowy night, clambering up a rope ladder to visit her, while she waited at the window – the scene gives a foretaste of the melancholy meeting of the lovers in *Pelléas*, although here perhaps more farcical than moody. One biographer all but suggests that the affair petered out because she became unattractively plump; it is more likely that her husband could no longer turn a blind eye. By 1890, Vasnier had made definite moves to delimit Debussy's involvement with his wife; the family moved home in Paris and changed its holiday residence, too. Debussy was not invited again to join them – and that was that.

DEBUSSY AND WAGNER

As Mme. Vasnier left his life as inspiration and mistress, the figure of Wagner was stalking with ever heavier tread. Debussy knew what he liked in women and had some idea of the direction of his music; but when it came to Wagner, he was far less clear on either his love-hatred or his debt of inspiration. The fact remains that, of all the other composers, Wagner is the one Debussy most often scorns, yet from whom he most often derives ideas.

Debussy was far too good a musican and innovator to overlook Wagner's impact. The seamlessness and atmospheric resonance of Wagner's writing were also suited to Debussy's music. On the other hand, Wagner was seen as an oppressor, partly for half-political reasons, for he was a German, and partly for aesthetic reasons, for his music was so overwhelming. The admirers and his detractors all agreed on one thing – Wagner's music demands an extreme response. The two sides of this love-hate mean that although in his writings and reported opinions Debussy became quite vehemently anti-Wagner, the homage to and exploitation of Wagner's rich genius was frequently discernible in his own work.

Debussy probably first heard Wagner at the Conservatoire in 1876, although he may have heard some of his music on the Côte d'Azur even five years before that; the first act of *Lohengrin* was heard in Paris in 1879, and in 1880 Debussy heard a concert of orchestral excerpts in Vienna, on his travels with the von Meck household. In his teens, he had gone with Lavignac to a performance of the overture to *Tannhäuser* – they ended up by being locked in, so great was their absorbtion in the effect of this music. By the mid-1880s he was writing to M. Vasnier in a famous expression of self-deprecation: 'I could make use of Wagner but I do not need to tell you how ridiculous of me even to try.'

The French were not unanimous in their rejection of Wagner – far from it: by then (in 1885) there was even a Paris-based newsletter (what would today perhaps be called a 'fanzine'), called the *Revue wagnérienne*. *Lohengrin* in its entirety was given its first Paris performance in 1887 – a performance postponed a few days following protests and demonstrations against it – and in 1888 and 1889 Debussy actually travelled to Bayreuth, home of the Wagner festival and shrine to the lovers of Wagner's music. There he heard *Die Meistersinger* and *Parsifal*, in both years, and *Tristan und Isolde* the second year. As late as 1894 he earned 1,000fr for playing and even singing the first act of *Parsifal* (not yet heard in France) at a private party.

'As late as'? It was during the 1890s, during the composition of *Pelléas*, that Debussy's outward attitude to Wagner turned to hostility. In a way, given the extraordinary influence of the score of *Parsifal* on the *Tristan*esquely-plotted *Pelléas*, it was almost inevitable that Debussy should create a smokescreen, not least for his own benefit. Moreover, the influence of this work in particular lingers in orchestral works 'as late as' *Le Martyre de Saint Sébastien* (1911) as well as in *Jeux* (1912–13). Both, interestingly, were composed in a hurry; it is as though, when he could not help himself, Debussy found in Wagner a lexicon of scraps with which he could write most easily. The same is true of the orchestral interludes that he was still composing, against the clock, during the first run of performances of *Pelléas*.

Despite the similarities of plot and title between *Tristan und Isolde* (1856/59) and *Pelléas et Mélisande*, it was the more shimmering, nebulous, later score of Wagner's last opera *Parsifal* (1877/82) that influenced Debussy more. He himself referred to the score as being 'lit from behind' and it is true that in this score Wagner achieves a world of subtlety and sound, of finish and flow completely different from that of the early operas such as *Tannhäuser* or *Lohengrin*, and even from The *Ring* cycle. Debussy was aware of this. Even as late as in 1914, in a review of a performance of *Parsifal*, and despite his usual public anti-Wagnerian stance here expressed by a need to give something of a parody of the plot, he could write of 'the musical beauty of the opera, which is supreme. It is incomparable and bewildering, splendid and strong. *Parsifal* is one of the loveliest monuments of sound ever raised to the serene glory of music.' And he called it 'a magnificent contradiction of *The Ring*'.

The composer Robin Holloway has written a sometimes

breezily conversational, sometimes bracingly technical and musicological account of the relationship between the two composers. One of his most interesting points is in the extent to which Debussy's attitude not only resembles that of the philosopher Nietzsche – moving from love to hate – but that many of the things Nietzsche said, and which he intended as the worst barbs with which to attack Wagner, become true, and flatteringly so, of Debussy. To Nietzsche (1844–1900), French culture was an urbane and spent, insipid force, and in one of his tirades he called his erstwhile friend Wagner 'the greatest miniaturist', a remark as full of insight as it was intended to be full of deprecation. He provokingly called Wagner 'a master who compresses an infinity of meaning and sweetness into the smallest space' and French Wagnerism as dedicated to 'all the femininity from the vocabulary of happiness' – intendedly venomous descriptions that can nevertheless describe the special genius of Debussy.

THE WOMEN OF THE 1890s

Debussy and the Vasnier family had separated by 1890 and the composer found himself lacking the encouragement of a good friend and without the excitement of that friend's wife as his mistress. Consolation was always at hand: he was not unfamiliar with the low-life of Paris, then at its most fulsome, as we know from the dance-hall and brothel art of Toulouse-Lautrec and Degas. But, Debussy was the man who in that questionnaire had said that the greatest happiness was to love – not 'to be loved' nor merely to make love. Debussy needed to feel his own heart beat. With the new decade, however, came new love.

The romanticism of his need to love is nicely caught by the fact that in April 1890 he penned his dedication on the title page of his projected opera *Rodrigue et Chimène* before a single note of the music was written. The dedication is to Gabrielle Dupont (1866–1945), known usually as Gaby – a lithe, green-eyed, lively young woman whom he had just met. On that first page he wrote simply 'To Miss Gabrielle Dupont', but, more than a decade later, at the time of the first performances of his completed opera *Pelléas*, he wrote upon her copy of the score, referring to the wistful love of the drama: 'To Gaby, Princess of the mysterious Kingdom of Allemonde. Her old devoted friend Claude Debussy. June 1902.'

She had been his muse and mistress for the first eight of

those twelve intervening years – through the composition not only of the two acts of the first abandoned opera but also of the *String Quartet*, a dozen songs and piano pieces, the *Prélude à 'L' Après-midi d'un faune'*, the three *Nocturnes* and, of course, *Pelléas et Mélisande* itself. She was a character: sexy, passionate as well as practical. They lived together, much of the time in an attic costing 120fr. a year and while he composed, and earned some money for arrangements and a bit of teaching, she worked in all sorts of occupations such as laundress or milliner. They enjoyed a happy life together at the composer's most frustrating time – caught as he was between awareness that he was on the verge of fame, and not actually having a penny to his name. All the same, they were also by far his most fruitful years.

The writer René Peter (1872–1947) had known Debussy since the mid-1880s and many years later wrote an article entitled 'Debussy and Love'. He shrewdly refers to Debussy's work as 'a superior form of escapism towards an ideal all the more eagerly sought as his real, daily life removed him ever further from it. This explains the role, at the same time considerable and unimportant, that women played in his life.' Peter had seen this at work; in the late 1890s, his brother's wife Alice had had a passion for Debussy. He describes Gaby as:

> ... *a blonde with cat-like eyes, a powerful chin and firm opinions. She looked after the domestic side – there was not much Mélisande in her – and that was quite a big undertaking, first of all because they were poor and secondly because Claude, being a large, spoilt child who refused to allow himself to be manhandled by life, indulged all his whims and was impervious to reason. ... He emptied his purse without stopping to think where the next day's dinner would come from. And while he was lost in thought in company with his genius, Gaby would be out raising money on knicknacks at some sordid pawnshop.*

Her devotion to him was not matched. Perhaps the lack of that Mélisande magic was too irksome, or perhaps Debussy always had a restless need for a new muse. At any rate, in 1892 or so, he asked one Catherine Stevens to marry him. She was the daughter of Alfred Stevens, a painter of Anglo-Belgian descent. Debussy dedicated the first set of *Fêtes galantes* to her. Peter describes her as 'one of the most radiant and charming figures to whom Debussy ever succumbed' and in his dry, friendly and wistful style relates what he calls 'this sentimental episode':

> *There can be no doubt of the mutual attraction that soon grew up between the composer and the young girl. In other circumstances Debussy would probably have tried to lead matters to some less than idealistic conclusion, but here he was dealing with a young woman of honour with whom there could be no question of love-making without marriage. And why not marry? I quote a passage from a letter she wrote me shortly after we met: 'He gave me proof of such disinterested love during the worst moments of a family crisis [illness and her father's faltering reputation and earnings], he whom people have called grasping, and he was so intelligent and he played me Pelléas, which he was working on. I would have married him, despite everything that was being said about him at the time [he was after all living with Gaby in a relationship scandalous to some even without its being on his part so 'open'] if I had not met Henry!'*
>
> *The end of the story can be guessed at. Henry was a brilliant young doctor, sincere and charming. . . . Claude was dismissed gently, to spare his feelings, but for some days he was inconsolable. Then he returned to Pelléas – and to Gaby, whose triumph was, as always, to be only temporary.*

At least one reason for her refusal was that, in her position, Debussy's well-known liasion with Gaby had been a shade too public. Her notes are harsher on Debussy than this account suggests. She refers to him as an eccentric. Her social standing did not give her the patience to be as loyal as Gaby, waiting for the success of *Pelléas*; nor perhaps did she have the love, for shortly afterwards she was married to the other man, rather more respectable than the down-at-heel young composer.

Undaunted – he was used to rejection and managed to be 'inconsolable' for merely 'some days' after all – Debussy continued his open relationship with Gaby. All the same, he continued this relationship as much as a springboard for other romances as for its own charm. One trouble was that with Gaby, devoted as she was, Debussy was reminded of his penury. He missed the comforts of middle-class, even aristocratic company – all the more so at a time when he could see that his music had the quality, eventually, to bring him both social standing as well as means. With Gaby he remained the bohemian; the genius perhaps, but the scruffy genius, scraping by, all the same.

The relationship with Gaby had a potentially tragic but nonetheless theatrical side. One day, she found a letter in the composer's pocket, a letter from Alice Peter, the estranged wife of René Peter's brother, a woman 'who knew how to flirt amusingly, and who, seeing him ready to adapt himself to the part of *cavalier servant*, was happy to draw out the episode as far as it would go'. Gaby did not like what she read. Drama followed, tears – and a revolver. Gaby tried to shoot herself. Debussy reports the events to his friend, confidant and occasional librettist, the writer Pierre Louÿs (1870–1925) in terms more vexed by the nuisance than by concern: 'This poor little Gaby has just lost her father, and this encounter with death has temporarily caused these ludicrous tales.' He manages to add, 'Nevertheless, I have been upset.'

Gaby and Debussy were reunited, but the incident temporarily strained the tolerance of some of the composer's friends, not least the composer Ernest Chausson (1855–99), one of his most treasured companions and the Belgian violinist Eugène Ysaÿe (1858–1931), whose quartet received the dedication and gave the first performance of Debussy's *String Quartet*.

In 1898 however, his relationship with Gaby ending if not ended, and with Alice Peter still in the picture but only just, Debussy met Rosalie Texier (1873–1932), known as Lilly, Lily or Lilo. Within eighteen months she was Debussy's wife. Mary Garden (1874–1967), the first Mélisande, left copious and sometimes fanciful memoirs of Debussy, but her account of the episode – for this, too, was ultimately only to be an episode – is succinct: 'Well, Debussy met Lily, fell in love with her, and she with him, and he left Gaby to marry her.'

In fact, Lily and Debussy were not together the whole time between meeting and marriage. They tried living together but the experiment was not a success. Gaby was friends both with Alice and with Lily and perhaps her example and her account of domestic experiences served to scale down the enthusiasm of the others. Late in 1899 they were engaged all the same – surely despite rather than because of Debussy's threats to kill himself if Lily refused him – and, with wry circumlocution, Debussy wrote to the publisher Georges Hartmann (1843–1900) to say that his summer had been unhappy but that he had had 'tender compensations, and I must warn you of my marriage with the aforesaid compensations.' Hartmann had been giving him an allowance of 500fr. each month, and considered him affectionately as 'that awful fellow'. It was to be, Debussy promised him, a marriage 'without foolish display and without bad music'. The marriage took place on 19 October 1899 and the witnesses included Louÿs and Erik Satie.

Satie, although he was more or less his exact contemporary (1865–1925), only met Debussy in 1891 or thereabouts, but was already known to him for his oddball buffoonery and occasional sense of quite surreal mischief, especially in his piano miniatures. It is said that his awkward character appealed to Debussy – reticent and shy despite a brash wit and strong ideas.

THE FRIENDS OF THE 1890s

Debussy was surrounded both by friends whose loyalty – or tolerance – fluctuated, and also by musicians, and others, of the highest distinction at the time, and whose standing has not diminished in the century since.

Among their number were Paul Dukas (1865–1935) and Gabriel Fauré (1845–1924). Dukas was more of a professor than a composer – although his brilliant orchestral scherzo *L' Apprenti sorcier* is indestructible in the repertoire and the relative neglect of his opera *Ariane et Barbe-Bleue* is unjustified – and he destroyed most of his unfinished music just before his death; but he was a trusted source of honest advice and resourceful support throughout Debussy's life. Indeed, as he composed *Pelléas*, Debussy refused to let Dukas hear his home performances of progress so far, telling him: 'I would much rather wait until I have finished an act or two to be able to give you a more complete idea of it. I hope that you will be touched by such self-denial and that you will find in it only a desire to please you better, for it is almost useless to tell you all the value I place upon your criticisms as well as upon your encouragement.'

As for Gabriel Fauré, he was as well-known as a teacher as he was as a composer, having taught composers as diverse as Ravel, Georges Enesco and Nadia Boulanger, as well as Koechlin, who was also a particular friend of Debussy's. Fauré wrote a suite intended as instrumental music for *Pelléas et Mélisande*, which was first heard (in London) in 1898. His music, so typically 'French' and, despite its clarity, opulent, does not, however have the underlying sting that exists in Debussy, nor the mischief; and nor did his character. His friendship with the younger man was not quite so consistent, strained especially by Debussy's waywardness.

Charles Koechlin (1867–1950) wrote posthumous studies of both Fauré and Debussy, having been by far one of the most conspicuous and understanding of his friends through his various misdemeanours. Valued as an accompanist, he had a mind perhaps more sharp in vision than in creative power; yet his songs have a charm that is immediate and satisfying. He was a particularly fine master of orchestration, yet Debussy turned most of all to André Caplet (1878–1925) to help him with this task, which, oddly, he himself seldom relished. Caplet had received the Prix de Rome in 1901, and in 1911 conducted the first performance of *Le Martyre de Saint Sébastien*; his own music is unashamedly impressionistic.

Debussy was also on generally good terms with Chausson, who died in a bicycle accident at a time when, it is true, his love of Wagner was proving an obstacle to Debussy. He was also a generous man of private means, and with Debussy that was itself a cause of ambivalent feelings. The ironies were compounded when Chausson helped Debussy out financially at the time of the composition of *Pelléas* – by having him play at private evenings designed to promote Wagner's music!

As for Vincent d'Indy, they had a cordial relationship. He too was a Wagner devotee and had even met Wagner, Liszt and Brahms in the early 1870s. Among his many writings is an introduction to the study of *Parsifal*. On the other hand, he also assisted in editing operatic works by Rameau and Monteverdi, and was sensitive to the importance of Gregorian chant at a time when that was – to say the least – unusual. In terms of French music he was more linked to the solid virtues of the music of César Franck than to the more mercurial muse of the younger composers. Nonetheless, there were gala concerts in 1917 that featured their music together. Fauré sent an invitation to Debussy, but he refused to attend, no longer able to face playing in public.

THE MUSIC OF THE 1890s

During these years, Debussy's knowledge of Eastern music deepened, partly through the various performances and exhibitions mounted at the huge *Exposition Universelle* of 1889. Technically, he was drawn to the harmonies of Eastern music, which, he could hear, could be made to work within the context of Western harmony. He was also drawn to the fact that Eastern music is less of a concert phenomenon – with all the superficial and competitive elements that that implies – and more of a spiritual, or contemplative, inner expression. Two things in particular struck him: the way in which Eastern music relates closely to physical expression such as dance (far more so than Western concert music), and its mood of avoidance of resolution. Debussy would have had in mind the delicate playing of the Indonesian gamelan when he said to Charles Koechlin, 'Our percussion in Europe is an art of barbarians.' One pianist wrote in this connection that 'Debussy regarded the piano as the Balinese musicians regard their gamelan orchestras. He was interested not so much in the single tone that was obviously heard when a note was struck, as in the patterns of resonance which that tone set up around itself.'

None of these aspects of Eastern music is alien to the true mission of Wagner's music; Wagner sought to suppress the usual conventions of 'performance' (in Bayreuth, the theatre designed by Wagner himself for the Wagner festivals, only the on-stage image was to be seen, the orchestra and conductor being hidden) to unite all art forms, including dance and drama, within 'music-drama', and, in *Parsifal* most spectacularly, to evade harmonic resolution in a seemingly endless ebb and flow of music.

Debussy had been working on *Rodrigue et Chimène* – another 'lovers'-names' opera – after the visits to Bayreuth, but he abandoned this in 1892. What he did complete of it was to wait nearly a hundred years for its first full public performance, despite the fact that Debussy himself played it privately thereafter and indeed despite the advocacy of musicians such as the pianist Alfred Cortot after the composer's death. (It is ironic that Cortot [1877–1962] was one of the leading champions of Wagner's music in France; he gave the first French performances of *Götterdämmerung*, in 1902, having worked as an assistant conductor at Bayreuth.) The text of the opera was by Catulle Mendès (1841–1909), an important writer who had supplied Chabrier with the text for his Franco-Wagnerian opera *Gwendoline* (1886) and to whom Debussy owed a debt, for it was Mendès who subsidized the engraving of the score of the *Fantaisie* for piano and orchestra.

Indeed, Debussy's inspiration was more to do with expediency than any true sympathy with the project. Any association with Mendès would bring him notice and make his music less likely to be neglected, and Debussy needed something of a proper big success at this time in his career. Yet, one friend described the text as 'perfectly void of interest'; nor after completing two acts could Debussy fool himself any longer, and he gave it up. He had, in his own words, 'won some victories over himself', but he was no longer prepared to fight his deeper instincts. He had adopted too much of an operatic stylization alien to his ear, in dealing with an arch and artificial love story. If he was to complete an opera, its mood, setting and passion would all have to suit him far more, especially his ultimately undramatic nature that was so far removed from the bit-by-bit sequence of intricate situation that characterizes opera.

When he played the score to friends, it made a very positive impression. (Did *that* help to put him off, however? He distrusted praise and on one occasion said that the only good music critic he knew was his contemporary, one Henry Gauthier-Villars Willy, who 'knows nothing about music. He does not know what a semi-quaver is, but he understands a composition.') Paul Dukas heard Debussy play and sing through 'his opera' in October 1893 – well after the date at which he had given up on it, all the same – and reported surprise at 'the dramatic breadth of certain scenes,' concluding with the dry and appropriate remark: 'Add that all the episodic scenes are exquisite and of a harmonic subtlety that recalls his early songs. Yet the work has everything that makes its failure certain. Let us wish that he might succeed!' This mood helped Debussy to the resolve that one day, not yet, but on a better text and with his fullest heart, he would write an opera.

He began work on that – on *Pelléas et Mélisande* – sooner than he expected, after closing the book on the Mendès text. Indeed, soon after seeing Maeterlinck's play for the first time, in May 1893, he had started, completing a 'first version' in two years. The final version, however, took until the end of the century, at least in theory, although from 1895 until 1901 he probably did only very slight spasmodic tinkerings, most of all to the final full work of orchestration. There was no substantial revision or reshaping.

In the meantime, he had worked on a wide variety of pieces, including short individual pieces for piano, some with traditionally Chopinesque titles (including a *Valse romantique* and a *Mazurka*), and more songs. His *Fantaisie* for piano and orchestra was completed in 1890 and the following year he wrote the first set of *Fêtes galantes*. (The second set was written in the heatwave of the summer of 1904, a present for Emma Bardac, who was to become his second wife.) Also in 1891 he wrote *Trois Mélodies de Verlaine*.

He was never utterly happy with the *Fantaisie* and even seemed glad to be able to cancel its first scheduled performance when it was suggested that the concert programme was too long and that perhaps only the first movement might be played. That gave him his cue and he withdrew the work altogether. Three days later, he sold the score for 200fr. to a publisher who then never released it, and indeed who sold it on to the firm of Hartmann five years later; even then, the engraved plates paid for by Mendès were lost, and the piece was never released in the composer's lifetime. He did not mind. In 1909 he wrote of its seeming 'like a rather ridiculous struggle between the two forces' of piano and orchestra.

There was no such problem with two other pieces from these years – masterpieces that remain cornerstones in Debussy's output: namely the *String Quartet* and the *Prélude à 'L' Après-midi d'un faune'*. Debussy made at least two false starts to resolve his problems with the *Quartet*, writing to Chausson in 1893 that he was starting from the beginning again for the third time, unable to 'get it as I want it to be'. All the same, in its finished form, Debussy's outdoor muse had its first greatest exposition, its breezy fashion evocative of the swaying leaves and patterns of Monet's trees by the riverside. Revealed, too, was his mischievous muse – the quartet opens with very definite, almost final cadences and exhibits one of his least dreamy, least languidly-constructed pieces of extended music. The sense of purpose throughout is unusual for Debussy – so much so that there is nonetheless a delicious tinge of irony about it as well.

With the *Prélude* on the other hand, there is a sultry heat, driving us oppressively into the shade rather than to carefree outdoor enjoyment; it is in fact a rather Roman sort of heat. The correct title of the work is *Prélude à 'L' Après-midi d'un faune'*; but it is sometimes referred to either just as the *Prélude* or by what is the title of the poem by Stéphane Mallarmé to which it is a 'prelude', *L'Après-midi d'un faune*. This is a poem of about 120 lines, an 'eclogue' in which the faun addresses nymphs and eventually stretches out in the heat, happy with the heady effect of wine. Debussy had known Mallarmé's poem for five years at least and had spent some time with the poet himself. The hazy heat of the music is an extraordinary and original creation. One commentator in 1900 gives a good picture of the inability of the public – and of the aesthetes – of the time, to know quite what was going on or quite where to stand:

> L'Après-midi d'un Faune *is one of the most exquisite instrumental fantasies which the young French school has produced. This work is too exquisite, Alas! it is too exquisite. The harmonic refinements and the perpetual modulations in which the composer delights, dwarf his work and make it flabby and insipid. I have no objection to an art being rendered intricate by daring and original innovations, but it must remain virile and human, otherwise it will only be of passing interest and can leave no lasting emotion. Pre-Raphaelism is already going out of fashion and its vogue amongst us was very short-lived, because it was utterly unsuited to our character and temperament. . . .*
>
> *M. Debussy has written the kind of music that suits the poem. I commend him for it and I consider that it is eminently successful. I wish he would now write music in keeping with the spirit and the genius of his race.*

The wilful jingoism of this criticism is revealing; it was written at the time of concerts given as part of the *Exposition Universelle* of 1900 in Paris, as part of an official report to the *Ministre de l'Instruction Publique*. The languid dandyism of French manners was evidently not what the government – and by extension, the military – wished to see as the finest espression of the national character. By then, Debussy had completed his opera, *Pelléas et Mélisande*, as exquisite and intricate as the *Prélude*, but on a huge scale, telling of exhaustion and defeat, and as French as France.

CHAPTER 3
PELLÉAS ET MÉLISANDE
(1893–1902)

♦ *Debussy's setting of Maeterlinck's play*

The relaxed tempo of action and inaction in Debussy's opera tells us much about his own creative needs. *Pelléas et Mélisande* was the only plot that drew immediate and sustained inspiration from him, and a synopsis of the plot may therefore be helpful here.

The plot and text of the opera follow Maeterlinck's original play quite closely. An exact contemporary of Debussy's, Maurice Maeterlinck was born in Belgium in 1862, and apart from *La Princesse Maleine* of 1889, had his first major success with *Pelléas*. His essays were published in 1901 under the title *Life of the Bees* and although in 1911 he was awarded the Nobel prize for Literature, he is read less nowadays than then.

The most startling aspect of the work – and we think of it nowadays as Debussy's rather than Maeterlinck's – is the presence of so much suffused eroticism and sexual imagery, close to the surface of what is otherwise a drama in which the frequently lurking characters seem almost devoid of either motivation or momentum. Furthermore, the eroticism has a nasty taste to it that is often overlooked, especially in the cruelty meted out to Mélisande by Pelléas's half-brother Golaud, to whom she is married. He is the only character of any dynamism in the entire drama, and yet, at the end, the accusation is made quite simply: 'You do not know what the soul is.'

PELLÉAS ET MÉLISANDE – SYNOPSIS
There are five acts, set in and around the castle of Allemonde.

ACT I In the first scene, Golaud appears, lost in a forest while out hunting. He hears sobbing, and comes upon a beautiful young girl, also lost. It is Mélisande; he persuades her to accompany him.

In the second scene, in a room in a castle, Geneviève, the mother of both Golaud and Pelléas, is reading a letter from Golaud in which he tells of how he met Mélisande and how he has now married her. He goes on to ask forgiveness of Arkel, his grandfather, who had had other plans for his marriage. Arkel is there as Geneviève reads, when Pelléas enters, requesting permission to leave to tend to a dying friend – but Arkel refuses: Pelléas's own father is dying and must take priority over a friend.

In the third scene, Mélisande and Geneviève are walking in the glades about the castle. Mélisande finds the place gloomy, but Geneviève shows her that light comes off the sea; they watch and Pelléas also appears from that side, announcing that there will be a storm and that he himself is preparing to leave. Mélisande can see that it was his ship that brought her there; sadly, she asks why he is leaving – but the act ends without a reply.

ACT 2   The second act opens at a fountain in the park. Pelléas is showing Mélisande the grounds of the castle. The sun is strong, the water cool. Pelléas questions Mélisande about Golaud (his half-brother), at the same time becoming enamoured of her long hair. She plays with the ring Golaud gave her and drops it into the fountain. They cannot find it. A clock strikes midday.

In the second scene, we are in Golaud's chamber; he is in bed after an accident – his horse threw him, on the stroke of midday, while hunting. He is confident that he will have his strength back soon, but notices that Mélisande has lost the ring. He is angry and she says that she knows where it is – that she dropped it in a cave by the sea. He insists he shall not sleep until she finds it, and insists, too, that Pelléas help her.

So, in the third scene, Pelléas and Mélisande are by the sea at the cave. It is dark. They can just make their way by moonlight. When a cloud disperses and the light is suddenly brighter, they see three figures sleeping in the cave; Pelléas explains that during the present famine these are likely to be peasants taking refuge. Pelléas and Mélisande creep out.

ACT 3   The third act opens in the late evening, at one of the towers of the castle. Mélisande is at a window, combing her hair and singing. Pelléas hears her and appears, begging her to let him see her hair – which she lets fall from the balcony. Pelléas enjoys playing in the luxuriant tresses when Golaud appears and scolds them for behaving like children.

In the second scene, Golaud has taken Pelléas to a damp vault, deep within the castle, to peer into a well. Pelléas has to give him his arm for support. Golaud's lamp swings a little. Pelléas is terrified. They leave.

In the third scene, Pelléas emerges from the vault onto a terrace, seemingly unaware of Golaud's suspicions. Golaud makes his warning plain this time: to leave Mélisande alone.

In the fourth scene, Golaud is still suspicious of the relationship between Pelléas and Mélisande; he is in front of the castle and questions his little son, Yniold, as to what he has seen them up to. His answers are enigmatic but clearly also suggestive. He describes their kissing by kissing his father, but is distressed by Golaud's prickly beard. A light goes on in Mélisande's room and Golaud has Yniold stand on his shoulders to watch. He tells of how the couple are gazing at their lamp – nothing more.

ACT 4   The action is tightened by having the scenes in pairs, the first two taking place in a room in the castle. Pelléas tells Mélisande that he is leaving. He has taken leave of his father, who is now feeling better but feels that Pelléas looks ill and likely to die and that he should therefore go away. Pelléas wishes to arrange to see Mélisande one last time, at the Fountain of the Blind.

Arkel appears; in a long aria he confesses that Mélisande's youth and beauty gives him hope, compensating for his approaching old-age and death. Golaud appears, and loses his temper with Mélisande, almost attacking her and seizing her by the hair. He leaves.

After an interlude, the third scene takes place at the fountain; little Yniold is playing, trying to move a boulder so that he can rescue a ball that has lodged itself underneath. A shepherd passes with his silent flock, evidently on the way to slaughter. Yniold runs off. Pelléas and Mélisande enter and here they declare their love. When they embrace, Golaud comes on and kills Pelléas. Wounded, Mélisande flees and Golaud gives chase.

ACT 5   The last act has only one scene, set in Mélisande's chamber; she is in bed, recovering from the wound. She has given birth to a little daughter and Arkel brings the child in for her to see. Mélisande dies. Arkel explains that Golaud has understood nothing – that now the little girl must live on in Mélisande's place. 'It is her turn now.'

CHAPTER 4
THE NEW CENTURY
(1901–5)

- ◆ Pelléas in preparation
- ◆ Pelléas performed
- ◆ First wife, second wife
- ◆ La Mer
- ◆ Spasmodic inspiration

The first year of the new century was also the first year of marriage for the Debussys. It was not happy. As it became clearer that *Pelléas* would certainly soon be performed, and as other works were receiving more recognition, Debussy's morale as a composer increased. In the summer of 1901, *Pelléas* was announced in the press for the next year and Debussy played it to Ravel. This much looked good. In the April, however, the publisher Hartmann had died, and with it the allowance that was still important to the composer's finances. The firm was taken over by a relative of Hartmann's – an army general, no less – who not only stopped the allowance but sought to reclaim some of what had been paid out. And in August, Lily lost their child they were expecting.

Debussy knew that all this was a mere faltering of fate before the great moment that was sure to come – but it was a miserable faltering all the same. Since completing *Pelléas*, he had written very little, partly exhausted by the rapid and relatively uninterrupted inspiration for that score, partly distracted by anxiety to see it staged and to receive his long-deserved major, indubitable success.

Only in the spring of 1901 was *Pelléas* finally safe; in April, Debussy played it to the director of the Opéra-Comique and by early May he had received a written assurance that it would be performed. Then, fresh troubles began, of course: he was confronted by a lot of last-minute work, for the orchestration was not complete and there was additional interlude music to be written to cover time taken for scene changes and so on – but all the same, it was work executed in the happy knowledge that the opera would at last be performed.

Performed – but how? Debussy had a very special sort of sound in mind, a new kind of relationship between text and music, as far from the lyricism of Italian *bel canto* as the work of Wagner was. One day, with the prospective cast to hear him, he played the opera through at the piano, and, though the assembled singers were reduced to tears, when he had finished Debussy simply said: 'Ladies and gentlemen, that is my *Pelléas et Mélisande*. To sing the music of Debussy you must forget that you are *singers*. Forget, I beg you, that you are singers. Good day.' With that he left the room.

Even finding his cast had posed problems. For one thing, Maeterlinck had wished his mistress Georgette Leblanc (1875–1941) to sing Mélisande, but Debussy was not completely convinced. She had sung Carmen a couple of seasons before and was more suited to a gutsy role of that sort than to the more slender vitality of a Mélisande. The matter rested there until Debussy came upon Mary Garden in the autumn of 1901– from that moment on, he was adamant that she and only she would create the role. Maeterlinck, who had actually managed to fall asleep when Debussy played the opera through for him, now awakened his deepest anger and stormed to the composer, demanding a change of mind – but to no avail.

The playwright's campaign for his singer continued even after rehearsals had begun in January 1902. It was a sorry spectacle and he was out-manoeuvred. Debussy reported with wry glee: 'Maeterlinck is in the bag, and Carré [director of the Opéra-Comique] shares my opinion that his case is pathological. But there are still mental hospitals in France.' This glee was to prove premature, for Maeterlinck pursued his case nearly to the courts, before being dissuaded. For her part, Georgette Leblanc's account of the episode includes the verdict of Maeterlinck on the subject of composers, whom he did not like 'any more than he did music': he declared to her, 'Those composers, they're all insane, all sick in the head!'

Debussy had certainly not wanted a fight with the playwright but even less did he want the premiere of his masterpiece in any way compromised. Nonetheless, things were to hot up that April. Tensions were building throughout the rehearsal period – understandably so – but the success of the first full dress-rehearsal helped to calm everyone down. Debussy was still writing the extra music to cover scene-changes that were so cumbersome in the cramped, old-fashioned theatre, but progress was good. (He was still working on these scenes at the end of the first run of performances, in late June.) Even Massenet, then sixty years old, heard some of the opera with evident admiration and emotion.

On 13 April, an announcement proclaimed that the first performance was to be on the 23rd. This was the match to Maeterlinck's short fuse. He wrote a letter to *Le Figaro* the next day, denouncing the whole production. Factually more or less correct in its version of various meetings, promises and undertakings, the letter nonetheless reeked of small-mindedness, and helped stoke a mood of controversy – scandal even – around the opera, which only assisted Debussy's celebrity.

The open letter ended:

> *In a word, the* Pelléas *at issue is a piece that has become a stranger to me, almost an enemy. And, deprived of all control over my work, I am reduced to hoping that its failure will be prompt and resounding.*

Controversy was assured. There could be no better advertisement for a new opera.

The last dress-rehearsal, something of a public event in itself, had a mixed, fairly quiet reception. That is to say, supporters and detractors of Debussy argued their cases with one another. All well and good. The conductor Henri Busser (1872– 1973), who took over after the first three performances, reported of this public dress-rehearsal: 'Success is assured with the fourth and fifth acts. Debussy takes refuge in Messager's office and nervously smokes one cigarette after another.'

There was a far more animated response, however, on the actual first night, on 30 April 1902. The net outcome of this was that Debussy had 'arrived'. His opera was the most talked-of artistic event of the season and tended to win over its detractors rather than lose him supporters. Performances continued and, as the *Le Figaro* reported, 'Each evening it wins a new victory with the public. . . applauded by the most famous composers.' Busser noted of the third performance that there was a 'large audience, more responsive and sympathetic. At the end there are calls for Debussy but he refuses to appear on stage.'

Intoxicated, too, by the excitement of the new century, many writers championed the opera as the triumph of the voice of youth over the establishment. It became an obsession, with people returning again and again. Just as good for Debussy's reputation was the opposition of the old guard, such as Saint-Saëns and members of the Conservatoire. René Peter remarked that he could well remember, at the third performance, the sight of the popular singer known as Paulus 'leaving the theatre in fits of laughter! This was the first sure sign of victory.'

Still, for Debussy, even this triumph was like an echo of just deserts now ten years in the waiting. Mary Garden recalls that he had a habit in life of 'suddenly walking out' from things, as he had from Gaby's life and was to do from Lily's; and as he did from *Pelléas*. 'It was after the last rehearsal that Debussy did the very characteristic thing of walking out of the life of Mélisande. He never came to a single performance of *Pelléas*. Again and again I asked him to come to watch the complete fulfilment of his dream, and one night he tried to make me understand. "Mary, I can't ever go," he said. "*Pelléas* is my child. I had it in my hands for ten years. I gave it to the public, and now it doesn't interest me any longer."'

AND THEN? – A NEW WIFE

By the time of the first performances of *Pelléas* – truly a dream come true – the undreamlike qualities of his wife were inspiring nothing more than boredom in the composer. One of Debussy's biographers makes it plain that the reason Debussy was able to conceive *La Mer* so precisely, while gazing out not upon the sea but upon the hills of landlocked Burgundy, was that, most of all, he was gazing in wistful desperation away from his 'little wife'. Equally, after *Pelléas*, his character may have undergone something of a change. Peter noticed 'unmistakable signs that from then on he began to leave us. Not that he changed; but despite him, despite all of us, he moved into a different category of being.' Whatever the explanation, this was a less productive Debussy than the composer of the 1880s, whose momentum had triumphed in *Pelléas et Mélisande*.

Certainly, his interest in the woman who was to be his second wife dates from the same time as the beginnings of his work on the symphonic tone poem *La Mer*. Emma Bardac, née Moyse, born in 1862, was from Bordeaux and was the mother of one of his pupils. Loved by Fauré, whose *'Dolly' Suite* was named after her daughter, she was very musical and had a combination of practicality and dreaminess that suited Debussy. Lily had never inspired him – a mere glance at the relatively uncreative years since the abandonment of Gaby shows this – but Emma did, immediately.

They met at a dinner held by her son for his teacher, in the autumn of 1903. Debussy was, of course, invited with Lily, who, during a subsequent illness, actually encouraged the composer not to worry with hanging around her while she recovered; he would be better off accepting dinner invitations. If he was reluctant, it was perhaps because he sensed that with Emma he had entered a gravitational field that would pull his marriage apart. Even while still married to Lily, he began to dedicate work to Emma – no less than six songs, in the spring of 1904; Lily could see that things were deteriorating.

Emma knew this too. Sending Debussy flowers in June 1904, she received a card of thanks in return, in which the composer describes how he had kissed each flower in turn, as though it were a human mouth. That month he completed and dedicated to her the second set of *Fêtes galantes*. On Bastille Day, Debussy left Lily and eloped with Emma. They went to Jersey, then to Dieppe.

Just as he was brave enough to return to Paris, Lily shot herself. Mary Garden received an anonymous note by messenger, saying she should go to a certain hospital in Paris; this she did:

> *They took me into a tiny room, and there lay Lily, with a bullet in her breast, wanting to die because her Claude had not come back to her. You must understand that this young girl never knew anything else in life but her love of Debussy. She took care of him like a child. They had worries and debts and disappointments, but nobody ever got into the little appartment of the rue Cardinet to interrupt Debussy at his music. Lily kept the world away, so her beloved Claude could work and be hers alone. As Lily lay there, pale and bandaged, she told me the story.*

She had seen Debussy's father, and he had told her that his son was in Dieppe, living with Mme. Bardac. 'I knew then, Mary, that he would never come back to me,' she sobbed.

Lily must have known her husband very well to suspect that if ever he made a decision he would stick to it. So she went out and got a revolver, and this beautiful young creature who had never held a gun in her hand, and didn't know how to use it, went into her bedroom and shot it off against the wall to try it.

Then she sat down and wrote Debussy a letter and sent it off by messenger in care of his father. She wanted the letter to be on its way at three o'clock, because at three o'clock she planned to kill herself and she didn't want Claude to get the letter until she had done the fatal thing to herself. Then she turned the gun on herself.

Debussy received the note and rushed round to find Lily on the floor; she had never lost consciousness. Unless he had come back to return to her, she announced, she wished to be left to die. He had her taken to hospital and asked if her life could be saved. The surgeon asked him to wait a couple of hours.

Debussy then took a seat in the corner of the waiting room, and with his hat on waited, like a bad boy in school, for the verdict. After two hours the surgeon came out. 'M. Debussy, we are happy to tell you that your wife will live.'

Debussy looked up at the doctor and in his husky voice muttered just one word: 'Merci.' And he walked out of the hospital and out of the lives of all of us.

The transition from Lily to Emma cost him some of his friends – understandably, perhaps, after such behaviour – as had the transition from Gaby to Lily. It was not helped by the fact that Emma was Jewish. Parisian society was still edgy after the Dreyfus affair had exposed the racist and anti-Semitic cracks in French society. Dreyfus, an Alsatian-Jewish officer on the General Staff, had been tried at a court martial in 1894, and convicted on what was suspected and later shown to be fabricated evidence. Such were the prejudices at work that it took five years for a retrial, held in 1895 as a result of extreme pressure from the press as well as demonstrations and even street fighting, and at which Dreyfus was merely pardoned; indeed, it took until 1906 for the formal acquittal. Throughout that time, the division between Drey-fusards – championed especially by the novelist Emile Zola and the politician Georges Clemenceau – and their opponents, the Army and the Church most of all, exposed a strong vein of antisemitism that ran through the whole of French society.

Even more than her race, Debussy knew also that Emma's relative wealth was quite an 'inconvenience': he was bound to be condemned for mercenary motives. And mercenary he was – but in another way – artistic and not financial. The fact was that Emma inspired him. The spring of 1905 was distracted by litiga-tion and 'meetings with some very tiresome people who are determining my fate', all to achieve a settlement with Lily. In May, Emma was divorced and by the August Debussy was, also. Emma and Debussy did not marry until 1908 but that summer, in 1905, they celebrated their togetherness with a trip to East-bourne, where Debussy found calm to turn his 'thinking machine' back towards composition. On 30 October their child Claude-Emma was born.

AND THEN? – NEW MUSIC

The story of *Pelléas et Mélisande* is not only the story of the focus of Debussy's success but also of his vacillation. Quite unlike Wagner, Debussy found that after so many years of hope, expec-tation and prevarication, the eventual triumph of his opera left him quite unsure of his next step. He faltered, dreading that he must now come up with something to match *Pelléas* and indeed to surpass it. Critics voiced the opinion that not only was that all he was capable of producing, but that other, younger composers could compose 'Debussy' better than Debussy himself.

It did not help that in terms of his inner progress as a composer, his opera was nearly a decade old at its first perform-ance. He was out of step with himself. Not long afterwards, he told a friend, 'If I had to write *Pelléas et Mélisande* all over again, I'd produce something quite different from what's played now.' The friend replied that that was what Gounod had said about his *Faust*, widely taken to be his masterpiece. To that, in good-humoured deprecation, Debussy simply said, 'Well, with *Faust* that's hardly surprising.'

Whatever he now wrote would have appear to have pro-gressed, even though (as the *Nocturnes* demonstrate) he had indeed progressed little by little. A project for a score for a production of *King Lear* did not materialize, nor had he succeeded in returning to a libretto entitled *Le Diable dans le beffroi*, based on Poe's *The Devil in the Bell-Tower*. He did complete the set of *Estampes* for piano, as well as the *Rapsodie* for saxophone and orchestra, all by late summer 1903. It was that autumn, however, that he was to find his next most substantial inspiration – the sea.

The sea does figure in *Pelléas*, of course, but with nothing like the shifting colours or restless – even positive – energy with which it assails the listener from the symphonic tone poem *La Mer*. Debussy had started to sketch this piece by September 1903 and, if only by its contrast with the melancholy tints of the sea scenes in the opera, it establishes his mastery over a quite different palette.

It is quite difficult to gauge sensibly the importance of the symbolism of the sea to the artistic world in France at that time. For this generation, the sea held an immense, poetic mystery. The novelist Alain-Fournier, whose first glimpse of the sea had not come until his teenage years, was not alone in enjoying the assonance between *la mer* and *la mère* – 'sea' and 'mother'. Debussy's own sightings of the sea – first as a boy on the Côte d'Azur – were events of far greater exotic moment than we might nowadays imagine. Moreover, there had grown, in the late nineteenth century, a passion for taking seaside holidays – and, more specifically, a passion, too, for seaside towns as the location for extra-marital affairs. All this was still quite new, and, of course, infested with inevitable class barriers.

There was for Debussy – as for the Impressionist painters – a fascination with the very colour of the sea. If Ravel is the musical painter of the sky – blue and fluffy-white in its gusts – Debussy is the painter of the green of the sea. Green was his favourite colour; and in his music, there is a sea rich in green rather than the conventional blue.

More often documented than his attitude to the Impressionist painters, is Debussy's love for J.M.W. Turner (1775–1851); and for that matter his love for James [Abbott] McNeill Whistler (1834–1903); there are no blue seas in Turner – all is green and restless. Indeed, the pianist Ricardo Viñes (1875–1943) records a conversation with Debussy in 1903, in which he remarked that *Pour le piano* made him think of Turner. Debussy replied that 'in fact, before writing them, he had spent a long time in the Turner room in London!'

Given the conspicuous lack of productivity for nearly a decade, the composition of *La Mer* was remarkably rapid, taking less than eighteen months in all. The whole piece, in three movements, was completed on 5 March 1905, and was dedicated to his good friend and shrewd publisher Jacques Durand (1865–1928). In the meantime, Debussy had written a number of piano pieces and songs.

The first performance of *La Mer* took place at the *Concerts Lamoureux* on 15 October 1905, to the usual mixed reception. (Charles Lamoureux (1834–99) was a conductor and violinist who had established this important concert season in 1881, not only to promote contemporary French music – but Wagner, too.) There was a flurry of articles and reproaches in the press, but the piece established Debussy in the more easily accessible – and more lucrative – repertoire of symphonic, orchestral music. The result was that, immediately afterwards, not only did other orchestras take up *La Mer* but also other pieces that had not before been widely performed. Even the *Prélude* had still been something of a rarity.

La Mer is such an extraordinary exercise in precision and energy, and Debussy's musical touch was a sure one – yet he was still unsure of his real direction. One unrelated success then another was too piecemeal, too static a progress for the man whose declared motto aspired 'Always Toward Higher Things'.

CHAPTER 5
YEARS OF
GROWING DARKNESS
(1906–18)

- ♦ *New difficulties in the search for an opera*
- ♦ *Projects abandoned*
- ♦ *Illness sets in*
- ♦ *A return to chamber music*
- ♦ *Outbreak of war*
- ♦ *Fading away*

The 'remaining years of his life'? It seems an odd expression to use of a man just turned forty and recently established with a fine international reputation. Yet something in his manner in the last ten or twelve years of his life (he was to die in 1918) is so listless and so unproductive that it is hard to escape thinking that he had lost interest in the continuation of his life.

His usual problems, in his home and in his financial affairs, were less urgent than ever; the former was especially happy. He was content as never before in his new 'marriage' – the actual ceremony only took place in January 1908 but the domesticity, routine, comfort and calm were well established long before. And he had an income both from royalties from *Pelléas* and in advances from his publisher. At any rate, to begin with, before 1910, he was able to live well and within his means. Too much so, perhaps? Around Christmas 1911 he wrote to André Caplet of his inability to fix his energies – and self-love – upon his music:

> *To sum up, one would have to suppress what consumes the best of our thoughts and arrive at loving only oneself with a ferocious*

concentration. Now it is the opposite that occurs: first, the family,
which clutters and obstructs me either with too much tender
concern or with a blind serenity. Then there come the Mistresses,
or the Mistress, upon whom one does not even rely, so happy is
one to give oneself to her, even to the point of oblivion.

Nonetheless, his chief consolation and by far the main source of
his happiness came from his young daughter, Chouchou. Much of
the finest music he was to compose came from inspiration more
or less directly responding to her and her early exploration of life.
However much the sequences of 'pictorial' piano music may owe
to Chopin or to Brahms on a technical level, or to the Impressionists on a pictorial level, they are also strong simply in their sense
of excited discovery of life's magic. The *Serenade for the Doll* is an
example of both these states of affairs, for it is a charming and artful
piece – but yet also the only complete composition from the year
1906. It is now known as No.3 of the suite *Children's Corner*, but
the other pieces were mostly composed in 1908.

Nor can it be said that fame spoiled him. He did become
accustomed to a rather more comfortable way of living than he
had ever enjoyed before – except at the hospitality of his early
patrons – but even that was only to last a couple of years. He
seemed to indulge in it because it was there, rather than with any
relish. True, he was certainly famous now, controversy having
largely given way to popular esteem and indeed stoking his
popularity; but, just as public expectation in the wake of *Pelléas*
quite simply frightened him, now the same was true again in the
wake of *La Mer*. The piano miniatures, masterpieces every one
of them, were a hard-won answer to this challenge on the small
scale. On the large scale he was less lucky.

He found that he enjoyed life in only a jaded fashion, rather
as if things were all a shade pointless; one writer dubs him a
condottiere retraité – a retired mercenary. He also found that, by the
same token, fewer of his friends enjoyed his company. He managed to fall out with Ravel and found himself altogether ill-at-ease
in the faction-ridden world of French music and musicians, what
he called – in print, what's more – 'a group of little republics
where each one exerts himself to make more noise than his
neighbour.' The article ends with a sentiment even more unlikely
to endear him to his old friends and colleagues. He wrote: 'It is

fortunate that no one in our day possesses talent, because it seems to me that that would be the most vexatious or the most ridiculous position imaginable in the world.'

Yet Debussy's fame was international and he was in demand. The enterprising man on the point of becoming the Director of the New York Metropolitan Opera, Giulio Gatti-Casazza, 'paid a visit to Debussy to pay my respects to him and to find out whether he had anything ready or in his mind. The composer received me in a very friendly manner and told me that he was really considering three compositions: *The Legend of Tristan*, *The Devil in the Belfry*, and *The Fall of the Houser of Usher* . . . but it was impossible for him to say when any one of these works would be ready for the theatre. . . . We agreed on a very small advance.'

Also among grand themes that Debussy dabbled with as successor to *Pelléas* was *Siddhartha*, a play along Buddhist lines by Victor Segalen (1878–1919). Whether or not Debussy knew that, after *Parsifal*, his demon Wagner had also considered Buddhist themes is uncertain; the possible irony is compounded, though, by the fact that Debussy was, in his turn, considering in some detail *L' Histoire de Tristan*, a project construed by Gabriel Mourey (1865–1943) from texts written by Joseph Bédier (1864–1938). Mourey was an art critic as well as a translator, who had known Debussy from before 1890 and who seems to have stolen the rights to the Tristan sketches from the vaudeville author Louis Artus (1870– 1960). Artus had obtained the rights from Bédier himself, to whom he was related.

Artus declared that he was happy to collaborate, but by then, Debussy was sufficiently self-important not to want to work with a man known as a hack playwright. He did want to work on a *Tristan* that drew from the French (and specifically the old Breton) legends. Various meetings ensued. Unhappy with Mourey's text and appalled at the idea of association with Artus, Debussy saw Bédier himself. But the latter had published his little *Histoire* in a rather disinterested fashion and, surprised – and unimpressed – by his own success with the book, had indeed signed away the rights and could not obtain them back from Artus.

The negotiations continued with ever-diminishing energy until well into 1910, before abating altogether. Wrangling of this sort helps to demonstrate how easily an artist could become jaded and gloomy in this squabblesome French artistic world.

Segalen, however, was a character of some depth, who worked not only as a writer but also as a diplomat. He was fascinated by exotic cultures – he had written a study of Maori music, for instance – and also wrote down notes from many conversations he had with the composer.

He gave an interesting account of Debussy in conversation on 8 October 1907, in note form:

DEBUSSY: . . . I've written *Pelléas*. So what? Pelléas! That gentleman's a bore! I wonder now if I'm not going to repeat him indefinitely. I certainly don't want to. It would be dreadful going over that again, or producing some equivalent in sound. I must go further. . . .

SEGALEN: Doubt is already some sort of response – ambiguous, but quite promising. And then, every creative, instinctive person has gone through times like that. How is *Tristan* coming on?

DEBUSSY: Mourey has read me the first act; which hangs together. And he's going to read me the rest tomorrow. This is the plan . . . of the scenes:

FIRST ACT

1) The King's bedchamber; the dwarf Froncin reveals that Tristan is the Queen's lover. Mark [the King] doesn't believe it. The proof. They are taken prisoner.

2) The lepers. Yseut abandoned among the lepers.

3) The hollow path. Tristan, unarmed, rescues Yseut. They escape.

SECOND ACT

The forest. The runaway couple are sad and tired of living in poverty.

THIRD ACT

The white moor. . . .

FOURTH ACT

1) Iseut of the White Hands.

2) Tristan's madness.

3) or 4) The treachery of Yseut of the White Hands – The Death of Tristan – and, which is excellent, 'My life is now too much to bear' —

DEBUSSY [*continues*]: Gabriel Mourey's prose is not very

singable, and there are many passages which don't exactly 'demand' to be set to music.

SEGALEN: Have you started on it?

DEBUSSY: No. I've still got to finish some things which don't want to be finished. Orchestral pieces which I can't bring myself to botch. I've never left anything unfinished so far. It's not something I want to do.

At any rate, a week after this conversation Debussy wrote to a friend that *Tristan* was indeed moving too fast for his taste: 'I have never understood the drive to work on the cheap, without wanting to look behind you, drawn on, moreover, by the thought of an utterly hazardous success.'

The conversation is interesting for light it sheds on Debussy's fictions about himself. He had added at the end that Segalen was 'one of the few people to whom I talk "music", or even to whom I talk about myself.' Perhaps. However, the last paragraph of his conversation, about leaving nothing unfinished, is not exactly true; in Lesure's catalogue of works by Debussy, the section *Projets non réalisés* has over fifty entries. One or two passages from Debussy's letters also start to weave a certain fabrication about himself – elsewhere, for instance, he claims that *Pelléas* took him a dozen years to write, although the premiere took place less than ten years after he had seen the play for the first time and less than seven years after he had completed the unorchestrated score. What purpose did these wishful little inaccuracies serve?

It is easy to see that he was not so much being mischievous towards his audience but that a touchingly pathetic effort was beginning in him, an effort towards self-delusion as a comfort against his extremely spasmodic inspiration in these years. This is more confirmed than belied by the fact that, when Debussy had seen Gatti-Casazza, apparently he confessed to being 'lazy', explaining that 'what is dominant in me is not talent; it is uncertainty and idleness. I am getting old and more idle than ever.' He was well aware of this crack and he knew how to paper over it. Three projects however did survive the difficulties of finding a suitable subject. One was *Le Martyre de Saint Sébastien*, and the other two were taken from works by Poe: *Le Diable dans le beffroi* – which he had already returned to immediately after the first performances of *Pelléas*, and *La Chute de la maison Usher*.

In the meantime, in the autumn of 1907 and on into the New Year, he worked on a second set of (three) *Images* for piano, to supplement the first set of 1904/05; and he continued on a set of pieces, also called *Images*, for orchestra. In 1908 he tackled the orchestration of his unimportant *Marche écossaise*, itself all but twenty years old but a good enough ruse to keep Durand, the publisher – and perhaps the composer's own self too? – under some sort of impression that progress was being made. Yet 1908 was a relatively productive year. He composed *Children's Corner* that year – more substantial and more simply poignant than any of his 'children's' music – as well as completing *Ibéria*, after almost three years of spasmodic work.

Ibéria belongs to the set of orchestral *Images* but has more often been linked, in concert and record programmes, with *La Mer*. The other two *Images* are *Rondes de Printemps* (given the number three but completed second, in 1909) and *Gigues* (origi-nally *Gigues tristes*, completed last, in 1912, and numbered as the first). None has the impact and subtlety of *La Mer* – and Debussy was all too aware of that. There was a popular taste for landscape music such as *Ibéria* – for concert showpieces and showcases of the composer's eye for atmosphere. Among these were Ravel's *Rapsodie espagnole* or Lalo's old warhorse, the *Symphonie espagnole* of 1875, but Debussy's is by far the most successful in its combination of joyous colour and oppressive heat.

ILLNESS SETS IN

It was in 1909 that Debussy made his first visit to the doctor, for any complaint probably connected with the cancer that was to end his life. Initially he had haemorroidal problems and was given a diet and a programme of exercise as well as cocaine and mor-phine. He certainly was left with little energy for his desk work and at times almost no particular desire to carry on life at all. He and his family had also spent their way into financial difficulty and he was forced to take on work that distracted him even further from composition.

Official recognition may not have helped him either, taking away any vestige of the rebellious youth that had launched him not so long before. Fauré encouraged him to take a vacant post on the Superior Council at the Conservatoire; he took it. The newspapers were bemused, but deep down Debussy hardly cared. He cared more for the conducting that he had started to take on, in London as well as Paris; at least there he could hide his need for the fees – albeit small ones – behind concern to 'protect' his music. He supervised the London premiere of *Pelléas* in the spring of 1909, for example, supervising scenery and lighting as well as the music, and contributing to a first performance that resulted in a frenzy 'that seems exceedingly rare in England, where the public's temperature usually remains below zero.' The frenzy was helped by the fact that during the dozen curtain calls at the end and the fifteen minutes clamour for the composer, Debussy was already back at his hotel.

By the autumn, his mind was back on the question of a libretto for an opera, in particular the Poe tale of *The Fall of the House of Usher*. He did a good deal of preparatory work for this, diverting some attention to a commission for a ballet from Diaghilev. He announced in late July that he intended to enjoy himself working on the ballet, and by late October had put aside the Poe completely, 'for this year at least'. He did find inspiration to work on a smaller scale later in the year, beginning the *Première Rapsodie* for clarinet, a competition piece for the Conservatoire, and, more importantly, the first book of *Préludes* for piano.

So, without focus but with some new music, he moved on to another year, 1910. He did not feel altogether as though any progress were being made, whatever the tremendous quality of the *Préludes*. He wrote to a friend that he was at a 'dangerous turning-point of his life', which seems more a reflection of the composer's continuing and unrelieved gloom and despondency than an accurate assessment of an actual crisis – except in his health, news of which was always distressing.

In 1910 he met Stravinsky, who enjoyed a mixed first few encounters with Debussy, beginning at the first performance by Diaghilev's *Ballets russes* of his ballet suite *The Firebird*:

> *I saw coming towards me Diaghilev and a dark man with a double forehead whom he introduced as Claude Debussy. The great composer spoke kindly about the music, ending his words with an invitation to dine with him. Some time later, when we were sitting together in his box at a performance of* Pelléas, *I asked him what he really thought of* The Firebird. *He said:*

'Well, whatever, you have to start with something or other.'

Honest, but not extremely flattering. Yet shortly after The Firebird *premiere he gave me his well-known photograph in profile with a dedication:* 'à Igor Stravinsky en toute sympathie artistique'. *I was not so honest about the work we were then hearing. I thought* Pelléas *a great bore as a whole, and in spite of many wonderful pages.*

Debussy liked to give Stravinsky presents, at one time a walking-stick with their initials intertwined as a monogram and, on another occasion, a cigarette case. Stravinsky remembered how he 'spoke in a low quiet voice, and the ends of his phrases were often inaudible – which was to the good, as they sometimes contained hidden stings and verbal booby traps.'

At the time of *The Rite of Spring*, in 1913 and after, the writer and doodler Jean Cocteau spread gossip that Debussy was 'tired of all these Russians' – meaning by that Diaghilev, Nijinsky, Stravinsky and the *Ballets russes* company – and their friendship was cooler. Stravinsky had never been all that taken by *Pelléas* but still, in 1969, in his late eighties, he returned to listening to 'portions' of it, telling his assistant and secretary Robert Craft, 'I like it better now than the last time I heard it.' He was asked when that was; 'When Debussy played it for me.'

Yet it is an indication of Debussy's sad state in these years that Stravinsky also had to note the 'impression that he was *not* especially interested in new things in music.' A similar sad tone is struck in another writer's recollection that Debussy praised Stravinsky's 'keen, fervent curiosity', saying nonetheless that it was 'good for young artists to be alive to new possibilities and to cast about, but that no doubt Stravinsky would sober down in due time.' This is not the young Debussy speaking – in his early days, he would have scorned such glum sanity – but the voice of an older, sadly self-doubting man.

The year 1910 was his worst for some time. His finances were in dire straits and on top of his own remorseless discomfort came the death of his father, in the October, after a long illness. He was in Vienna shortly after losing his father, hating every moment away from home, when Gabriele d'Annunzio wrote to him to suggest the text of *Le Martyre de Saint Sébastien*. Without enthusiasm, and without even seeing the text, Debussy agreed.

D'ANNUNZIO, DIAGHILEV AND THE DANCERS

D'Annunzio (1863–1938) was an Italian writer, champion of Symbolism and of a cult of beauty and refinement. His writings, still rather precious, have held up longer than those of Maeterlinck's, however, but he fancied his genius extravagantly. He took Debussy by storm with an 'irresistible whirlwind' of energy. It was, however, just as well Debussy had been convinced by the man without reading the text, as the enterprising (and penurious) d'Annunzio had not yet actually written a word. The first part arrived in January 1911 and Debussy plunged into a fever of industry. It must have been an extraordinary new feeling for him at that time. He also played in concerts, after one of which a critic wrote of his rendition of some of the *Préludes*, that 'his forthright and delicate playing may rightly be praised; he was given a loud and surpassingly long ovation.'

It was, however, the momentum of a headlong rush towards disaster. Far too much music had to be written in far too little time and the text of *Le Martyre* turned out to be poor. But the commitment was in place and there was a timetable to be kept to. After so much searching for an operatic libretto, it was ironic that Debussy had agreed to this without seeing the text, because clearly the success of the music – it is full of extraordinary beauty – was inspired by his own reaction just to the idea, free of constraints later applied by a text he thought was bad. Had he seen the text he might never have written the music and we should be without one of his most fascinating scores; how true might that be of all those projects abandoned or never started?

All the same, the whole business left him restless and exhausted that summer and into 1912. Nevertheless, unsure of the continuity of his inspiration as he was, 1912 saw the completion of a second set of *Préludes* for piano and the – relatively quick – composition of *Jeux*, a ballet for Diaghilev and Nijinsky that is, for many, his masterpiece of orchestral writing. This may be surprising, since the first proposed scenario he received from Nijinsky (fresh from the scandalous success of dancing the *Prélude à 'L'Après-midi d'un faune'*) was, he said, 'idiotic'. Originally, Nijinsky had wanted to give Diaghilev a ballet based on Diaghilev's dream of making love with two boys, but he had to change the two boys into girls. The resulting scenario is that a tennis ball bounces across a clearing in a park, and the man, rushing on in pursuit, comes across the two girls; they flirt and embrace until a second tennis ball lands among them and disperses their passion. Debussy had a point. With mischievous irony or simply in a rush to finish the piece (and earn the fee of 10,000fr), he took a good deal of well-concealed inspiration from *Parsifal* – from the scenes in which hapless the Parsifal falls among the Flower-maidens in the magic garden of the evil sorcerer Klingsor.

Jeux has fared better on the concert platform than as a ballet. It is a remarkable score. Not only is it musically a surprisingly neglected and rich masterpiece but it is unexpected in its histori-cal context. Diaghilev's *Ballets russes* had already worked with Stravinsky on *The Firebird*, and was poised to unleash *The Rite of Spring* (in 1913). The company was establishing a repertoire that can now be seen to encapsulate the feverishly suppressed vio-lence, the ritual panic of the times, as nations braced themselves (and equipped their armies) for the war to come. To set a game of tennis to music seems a typically sad defiance from a Debussy who could only relish the well-hidden, ironic references to that steamily threatening scene from *Parsifal*.

What is more, Debussy was now suddenly in a mood to complete things, including *Gigues* (for the set of orchestral *Im-ages*), and in the summer of 1913 he finished his final set of songs, the *Trois Poèmes de Stéphane Mallarmé*. Whether this mood belongs to his own health, the cancer within him taking hold, or has to do with the self-destructive buzz of the Europe around him, is hard to tell; probably both. He also indulged once more in a spate of travelling, to Moscow, Rome and the Netherlands, between late 1913 and the spring of 1914, as if 'before it was too late'.

War broke out in the summer of 1914; the Austrian Archduke Ferdinand and his wife were assassinated in Sarajevo on 28 June. A rattle of declarations of war followed; by 3 August, Germany had declared war on France and had invaded Belgium. Within months the Western Front had been established along the Marne and there was little fluctuation of the line for a period of three and a half years.

To begin with, the war brought fright and despondency to Debussy as to most of those who could not summon enthusiasm and patriotic relish. The privations stopped what little work he was doing, as did trials and tribulations, and he moved from Paris to the relative safety of Angers, to the west. The scale of the war seemed to Debussy to make writing music a 'wretchedly petty' activity. Yet it was in these years that he planned a sequence of six chamber sonatas, of which the three he lived to complete have a power and touch that make them his finest.

The war inevitably reduced the scale of the music it made sense to write. To help him earn some much-needed money, Durand asked him to edit the works of Chopin. This was a joy to Debussy. Intimate proximity inside the works of one of his most beloved composers had a tremendous effect. The textures and clarity that he knew so well fascinated him all the more for the extent to which it was a voyage of discovery, for the extent he did *not* turn out to know them as well as he had thought. This exploration and excitement also prompted him to write the *Études* for piano. Chopin's 'studies' are in two sets of twelve and Debussy wrote his as a set of twelve – and dedicated it to Chopin.

His mother died in 1915. Everything around him seemed in a state of collapse and self-destruction. Until the war, he had disliked being away from home – now he wished to flee Paris. For the summer he was given the use of a house at Pourville, near Dieppe – he loved the house, the garden and the sea view so deeply that he longed to have been able to buy it. Here he could work; here he could soak in the tranquil, anonymous wisdom of the sea, while behind him, the mad world was tearing itself apart in a sea of mud.

The last composition Debussy wrote was the *Noël des enfants qui n'ont plus de maisons*, 'The Christmas of children who no longer have a home'. Unusually, he wrote the words as well as the music and quite apart from continuing his special sympathy with the world of children even through the destructive circumstances of war, it has a poignancy within his own life. He had lost both his parents now, and his own attitude to his home had changed. Cancer of the colon had been diagnosed the previous month and Debussy, in continuous and peculiarly discomfiting pain, could see his home as a hospital, as well as where he would die.

He certainly had no reserves of strength or morale with which to fight his illness and upon hearing the diagnosis, he wrote to Fauré that he had suffered like a dog ever since. Clinical diagnosis of cancer, as often happens, comes after the inner realization has already taken place. He realized it in his work too. Before the round of appointments and investigations that November, he had

had a flurry of inspired work, the first for a year, which he described to a friend: 'I wrote like a fury or like one who is doomed to die the next morning.' This sense of exhilaration, of the value to be found in sparse resources, is the stamp of the late sonatas, with their edgy, fragmented elements and their anxious humility.

In January 1916 he wrote to Fauré: 'I am still, to my great regret, in the hands of some surgeons, physicians, and other assassins. Although they measure out the truth to me in very small doses, I am much afraid of being laid up for one more month by these deplorable events.' Clearly the doctors had told Debussy that hope and some patience would see his illness off – but he was short of both. He loathed the calls to be patient, for they simply served to remind him how much time in his life he seemed to have frittered or wasted unproductively. He became very pale and emaciated.

The summer brought an unsatisfactory holiday on the Atlantic coast, and Debussy longed, instead, for the little house at Pourville, overlooking the English Channel. But the break allowed him to begin work on the *Violin Sonata*, a work which, quite apart from the masterpiece it delivered, also gave rise to a glint of optimism about his health. He worked and worked and seemed all the better for it. This hardly lasted. His account of his days in December 1916 is of pain and sleeplessness, the pain and discomfort too much for him to sleep properly, yet he was also too tired to do much while awake. A feeling of futility set in. The rest of his life was to be spent in this oscillation between ever more pointless hope and ever more realistic gloom.

Work kept him going. He continued his duties at the Beaux-Arts and after one of the meetings confided to a colleague, 'I am not at all well. Positively, I believe that there is only time to work. I would like to hatch something fantastic, something devilish but vivacious, with much sweetness and light around it.' There are moments of this in the *Violin Sonata*; even more moving, though, are the powerful moments that express not so much the presence of such relief from pain and fear but the huge human need that there is for such relief.

The *Sonata* for flute, viola and harp had been completed in 1915, as had the *Sonata* for cello. The three sonatas were conceived as part of a set of six that he did not live to complete. Others only projected had unusual combinations of instruments:

oboe, horn and harpsichord or trumpet, clarinet, bassoon and piano. In the threesome of the flute, viola and harp, the first and last instruments in particular are associated with moody joy and breeziness, which adds to the sultry ironies of the dark colours that Debussy achieves. The risk is always present, the stage always ringed with barbed-wire.

The sonatas were not at first appreciated, partly because their classical title led to more conventional expectations, and partly, too, because of this lingering, elusive sense of threat. The extremities both of war and of illness seemed to give him an understanding of clarity that, even at its seemingly most joyous, has an almost frightening quality.

By the end of 1917, Debussy was hardly ever able to leave his bed and indeed could not properly sit up in bed. He was not strong enough to be carried to shelter during the air-raids that the Germans made in their final offensive in the spring of 1918. At last he had been persuaded to submit his candidacy for the Académie and he signed the letter the day before he died. On the evening of 25 March 1918, after a peaceful day in ever-deeper sleep, Debussy died.

He was buried on 28 March, at Père-Lachaise cemetery, but his remains were later transferred to the cemetery at Passy. His beloved daughter 'Chouchou', the treasure of his married life, was soon to follow; she died of diphtheria in 1919.

CHAPTER 6

DEBUSSY ON RECORD

Debussy's work is listed here according to type. Catalogue numbers have not been given, because some recordings come in and out of circulation at an alarming speed, each time with a new number. And any serious music-lover should not be too proud to consider second-hand compact discs, nor too devoted to technology to disdain second-hand long-playing records. It will become clear that I personally place musical values above those of sound quality, finding the cleanness achieved so impressively in the recording studio to be, as often as not, an emotional anaesthetic.

I have given dates of recordings and details of record companies in most cases, but any decent shop can locate a record referred to by the title of the piece and the name(s) of the performer(s).

Not surprisingly, a good number of recordings survives by artists whom Debussy knew and even by musicians who had studied their interpretation with him. Indeed, the surprise is that we might have expected there to be more. We might certainly have expected Debussy himself to have made more – but in the end he made only four, all as the accompanist to Mary Garden.

As a pueformer, or when advising on interpretation, Debussy himself was capable of being extremely demanding or easy-going, depending on his mood; both attitudes were encouraged by the fact that he was certainly a shade cynical about the chances of good performance in any case.

A performer of Debussy's music – the chamber and piano music most of all – is faced with a plain dilemma. One approach is the creation of a wash of sound evidently apt if that is how one sees Impressionism, as a haze with soft or indistinct edges. The other is a clarity and precision that would more usually be associated with the harpsichord textures in Rameau or Couperin. In general, it seems likely that Debussy preferred the latter – and that performers have not followed this.

OPERA & SONG

The same dilemma faces interpreters of *Pelléas* and the other operatic projects and cantatas and so on. When Debussy told the first cast of *Pelléas* that they should forget that they are singers, he meant both to forget the demeanor of grand opera but also the declamatory voice itself. He wanted song to seem more spoken and the rhythms of speech to be unveiled as deeply musical.

*Un*veiled? – It is important to shy away from the idea of veiling things in Debussy's music; he requires clarity, and what is played clearly will achieve all the required effects of veiling and haze. Thus I have found the recording of *Pelléas* by Charles Dutoit (Decca) too heavy-handedly and uniformly mysterious, and the even quite clinical sound of Serge Baudo (Erato) – harsh as it may seem at first – is all the more varied and, when mysterious or edgy, extremely so. On record, the tradition of almost analytically clear detail in this work may have been started by Pierre Boulez (CBS), and his version is still important and strangely beguiling despite itself, with George Shirley and Elisabeth Söderström as the two lovers. The opposite tradition is at its most sumptuous with Herbert von Karajan (EMI), with a rich beauty of sound that is hugely lush and an extraordinary attention to verbal detail, but which after a while seems smug and ultimately utterly at odds with the drama.

Oddly, older recordings of *Pelléas* can acquire greater theatrical presence, greater ranges of shade and shadow, by dint simply of their less strident sound. For this reason, if forced back to only one version, I should not want to part with the version by Roger Désormière (EMI, 1942), reverent and moving as it is. The later of Ernest Ansermet's two recordings has an almost equally irresistible quality (Decca, 1964).

The earlier Ansermet version (Decca, 1951) has the serious disadvantage of a cutting, nasal Pelléas, just as the Fournet set (Philips, 1953) is let down by the Mélisande. His later recording is hugely satisfying, however. Two recordings suggest themselves because of the interest of their Mélisandes, the 'live' performance with Elisabeth Schwarzkopf, under Karajan (RAI Rome, 1953) and one conducted by André Cluytens (World Records, 1957; Testament), with Victoria de los Angeles.

At the time of writing, *Rodrigue et Chimène* is available on only one issue, from Erato, conducted by Kent Nagano. It will not be easy to better this. With only a little less enthusiasm, much the same has to be said of *Le Martyre de Saint Sébastien* in a recording from CBS-Sony under Michael Tilson Thomas.

On CD, the Désormière *Pelléas* has been reissued (EMI Références), along with songs and arias sung by Mary Garden (with Debussy) and Maggie Teyte (with Alfred Cortot) and these glimpses of other singers are irresistible, the Teyte especially. For Debussy's songs we still have to sift about from one or two here and there. No satisfactory complete set has been made and indeed few records are devoted to Debussy alone. Exceptions come from the underrated label Etcetera, with Anne-Marie Rodde and Noël Lee; and from Unicorn, with Claudette Leblanc and Valerie Tryon.

Given that Hyperion has continued an important series of French Song recordings (including so far fascinating, unusual records devoted to Reynaldo Hahn, Charles Koechlin, Henri Duparc, Lily Boulanger), can Debussy have long to wait?

ORCHESTRAL MUSIC

The French tradition has much going for it – and much against it. On EMI alone, in various overlapping selections, there are Simon Rattle in Birmingham and von Karajan in Berlin as well as Erich Leinsdorf in Los Angeles, Riccardo Muti in Philadelphia and a bundle of authentic French line-ups such as Jean Martinon, Serge Baudo and Michel Plasson. In general, the non-French are more investigative and best at making you hear a well-known piece afresh; and the French are best for creating the mood that Debussy expressed when he said to a conductor who wished to consult him on detail after detail of a score: 'I don't mind; you know what to do.' Recordings by Ernest Ansermet and Pierre Monteux are the most exceptional in this regard, even if their sound does not have the often distracting 'presence' of contemporary taste. Let me also register that for *Ibéria*, the Leopold Stokowski version (EMI) is exceptional.

As is Toscanini in *La Mer*, most of all in a 'live' performance with the BBC Symphony Orchestra, recorded in London in 1936, with music from Wagner's *Parsifal* also exceptional (EMI Références). Toscanini is a special case – he worked with Debussy for the Italian premiere of *Pelléas*, an opera that he championed but never recorded. There is a recording, intermittently available, of a broadcast concert he gave in 1940, entirely devoted to Debussy, which includes a fine account of *La Damoiselle élue* as well as *Ibéria*, *La Mer*, and some shorter pieces. Given Toscanini's reputation for harsh sound and a pernickety ear, it can seem strange that his Debussy is so satisfying – until you recall the theory that the composer was looking for the 'impressionism' to make itself heard without help.

CHAMBER MUSIC

Almost every quartet records the *String Quartet* – not all equally well. The Lindsays (ASV) are better than most, a very gripping account, as is that of the Juilliard Quartet (RCA). An old record of the Parrenin Quartet (EMI) has a fine flavour to it. Nobody is as fine as the Quatuor Capet (EMI Références), records made in 1927 and of simply thrilling subtlety and energy. No other version seems to understand so vividly what is at stake.

A tremendously good record comes from Pearl, with old performances of the *Violin Sonata* (Thibaud & Cortot), the *Cello Sonata* (Maréchal & Casadesus) as well as the late *Sonata* for flute, viola and harp. The devotion of these performances is haunting and – like the Capet – it is one of those few records after which you find you want to play it again immediately.

Not many contemporary violinists match Jacques Thibaud and Alfred Cortot in the Violin Sonata (EMI Références; and Pearl). Yehudi Menuhin is one (EMI); he understands the 'off-hand' gestures of the part so well. The *Cello Sonata* has fared extraordinarily well, better even than the *Violin Sonata*. Notable versions even within that high standard come from William Conway & Peter Evans (Linn), Marc Coppey & Eric Le Sage (K.617), Maisky & Argerich (EMI), Rostropovich & Britten (Decca).

In 1970, the Boston Symphony Chamber Players recorded the three late *Sonatas* (DG) and it is an interesting opportunity to hear Michael Tilson Thomas as pianist. The *Violin Sonata* is good, with one of the too rare appearances by Joseph Silverstein.

PIANO MUSIC

The following pianists have recorded more or less complete sets of Debussy's piano music: Walter Gieseking (EMI Références), Robert Casadesus (CBS), Samson François (EMI), Claudio Arrau (Philips), Werner Haas (Philips), Peter Frankl (Vox), Lívia Rév

(Saga; Hyperion), Monique Haas (Erato), Aldo Ciccolini (EMI), Zoltán Kocsis (Philips), Paul Crossley (CBS-Sony), Mitsuko Uchida (Philips), Stany David Lasry (on a 1921 Erard; Arcana), Gordon Fergus-Thompson (ASV) and Martin Jones (Nimbus). There may be others and there seem certainly to be more to come.

One rule of thumb is that 'Debussy specialists' tend to have less flair than the pianists who are also at home in Chopin in a special way (François, Arrau, Kocsis for instance) – making it all the more a huge shame that Cortot recorded hardly a note of Debussy's solo piano music. Of earlier recordings, Gieseking's old set has a legendary status that endures, even if the vision of Arrau in particular is more challenging. I have always loved the playing of François, and although his Debussy is not quite the untold splendour of his Ravel, it reveals itself afresh again and again in passion and detail. Of more recent versions, Rév on Hyperion has the edge. Uchida, I find, is narcissistic. Fergus-Thompson's honesty, at first hearing plain, can then suddenly unearth the robust side of Debussy's art in an arresting way.

Individual records of distinction come from Boris Berman (Chandos) and, of course, Sviatoslav Richter (DG, Pyramid, etc.), his astonishing touch unrivalled by anyone – with the possible exception of Michelangeli (DG), whose greater clarity is perhaps more strictly what the composer thought of. An old set of Dino Ciani (DG) in the *Préludes* remains very special and the relatively recent set by Krystian Zimerman (DG), in glorious sound, is thought-provoking.

The *Préludes* in particular attract separate issues from some pianists: an old RCA set by Leonard Pennario is freshly thought-through. Most arresting of all however (other than Richter, Michelangeli and Zimerman) is Friedrich Gulda on BASF, wiry and lean, excited versions on an old LP which may require – but will certainly reward – a hunt. Not everyone records even a complete *Cahier*, and among selections I admire especially is a group of eight by Heinrich Neuhaus (Melodiya).

Marco Polo have issued a disc of Debussy's arrangements for piano duet, which includes the overture to Wagner's *Flying Dutchman*, and on Arion there is a pair of André Caplet's transcriptions for piano duet, of *La Mer* and *Ibéria*.

CLAUDE DEBUSSY: COMPLETE LIST OF WORKS

Works are given here in chronological order of completion. Within each year, the order is generally that of the numbers in the 1977 Lesure *Catalogue de l'oeuvre de Claude Debussy*; these are given as 'L' numbers; L. Ann.IV indicates the section of the catalogue devoted to 'Projets non réalisés'. Particularly important works that have been documented, but which were abandoned or never even started, are listed at the end of each year. Dates of first performances and some significant dedications are given for major works.

The details are given in the following order:

- *Title* (in italics)
- Instrumentation
- Dedication
- Date of composition (if the work took a particularly extended time)
- Author of text (where appropriate)
- Lesure catalogue number
- Date of first performance
- Finally, in parentheses, the date or dates of first publication
- If no date of publication is given, the piece exists only in manuscript or copies thereof

In the case of groups of pieces, the general details are given before a numbered list of the component pieces. Any date in brackets is a date of publication, all others being dates of composition or completion. In non-vocal music, mainly in certain piano pieces, the names of poets or writers in brackets indicates that Debussy had a certain text by that writer in mind, not only for the character of the piece but also sometimes in the title as well.

1879

Ballade à la Lune; for voice & piano; text by Alfred de Musset; L.1

Madrid, Princesse des Espagnes; fragment for voice & piano; text by Alfred de Musset; L.2

1880

Trio in G, for piano trio; to Émile Durand; L.3; (1986)

Nuit d'Étoiles; for voice & piano; text by Théodor de Banville; L.4; (1882)

Caprice; for voice & piano; text by Théodor de Banville; L.5; (1966)

Danse bohémienne; for piano; L.9; (1932)

Aimons-nous et dormons; for voice & piano; text by Théodor de Banville; L.16; (1933)

1881

Fleur des Blés; for voice & piano; text by A. Girod; L.7; (1891)

Symphonie in B minor; for piano duet; to Mme. von Meck; L.10; (1933; 1965)

Zéphyr; for voice & piano; text by Théodor de Banville; L.12; (1932)

Ouverture de Diane; for two pianos; text by Théodor de Banville; L.12*bis*

Rondel chinois; for voice & piano; text by unknown writer; L.17

Tragédie; for voice & piano; to Mme. Vasnier; text by L. Valade, after Heinrich Heine; L.18

Jane; for voice & piano; to Mme. Vasnier; text by Leconte de Lisle; L.19; (1966, 1982)

Hélène; for chorus; text by Leconte de Lisle; L.20*bis*

Rondeau; for voice & piano; text by Alfred de Musset; L.30; (1932)

La Fille aux cheveux de lin; for voice & piano; to Mme. Vasnier; text by Leconte de Lisle; L.33

L'Archet ; for voice & piano; text by Charles Cros; L.46

Chanson triste; sketch for voice & piano; text by Maurice Bouchor; L.47

Fleur des Eaux; sketch for voice & piano; text by Maurice Bouchor; L.48

Eglogue; for two voices; text by Leconte de Lisle; L.49

Les Baisers; for voice and piano; to Mme. Vasnier; text by Théodor de Banville; L.55*bis*

Les Elfes; for voice & piano; text by Leconte de Lisle
Les Papillons; for voice & piano; text by Théophile Gautier

1882

Séguidille; for voice & piano; text by Théophile Gautier; L.14
Daniel; cantata; text by E. Cicile; L.20
Fantoches; for voice & piano; (later version in *Fêtes galantes*, Set
    One; 1891/92; L.80); to Mme. Vasnier; text by Paul Verlaine;
    L.21
Salut printemps, originally called *Le Printemps*; for women's
    chorus & orchestra; text by the Comte de Ségur; L.24;
    (1928, for piano; 1956, for orchestra)
Flots, palmes, sables; for voice & piano; text by Madeleine
    Renaud; (harp accompaniment in manuscript separately as
    Mélodie persane); to Mme. Vasnier; L.25
Nocturne et Scherzo; for cello & piano; L.26
Intermezzo; for cello & orchestra; (Heinrich Heine); L.27;
    (1944, version for cello & piano)
Calmes dans le demi-jour; for voice & piano; (early version of *En
    sourdine*, from *Fêtes galantes*, Set One; 1891/92; L.80); text by
    Paul Verlaine; L.28; (1942, 1944)
Mandoline; for voice & piano; to Mme. Vasnier; text by Paul
    Verlaine; L.29; (1890)
Clair de Lune; for voice & piano; (later version in *Fêtes galantes*,
    Set One; 1891/92; L.80); to Mme. Vasnier; text by Paul
    Verlaine; L.32; (1926, 1969)
Choeur des brises; sketch for choir; text by Louis Bouilhet; L.35
Andante cantabile; for piano duet; L.36*bis*; (1987)
Sept Poèmes de Banville; for voice & piano; 1882 unless otherwise
    stated; (1984): 1) *Rêverie*; 1880; 2) *Souhait*; 1881; 3) *Le Lilas*;
    4) Sérénade; 5) *Il dort encore*; (scene I of *Hymnis*; see next
    entry); 6) *Les Roses*; 7) *Fête galante*
Hymnis; some scenes from incidental music for orchestra; text
    by Théodor de Banville; L.37: (includes *Il dort encore* from
    the entry before; and the next entry)
Ode bachique; for 2 voices & piano; (scene VII of *Hymnis*; see
    previous entry); L.37
Triomphe de Bacchus; suite in 4 movements for piano duet, also
    orchestrated; (Théodor de Banville); L.38; (1928; 1987):
    1) *Divertissement*; 2) *Andante*; 3) *Scherzo*; 4) *Marche & Bacchanale*

1883

Invocation; for men's chorus & orchestra; text by Alphonse de
Lamartine; L.40; (1928, version for piano accompaniment;
1957)

Le Gladiateur; cantata; text by Gustave Moreau; L.41

Chanson espagnole; for two equal voices & piano; text by Alfred
de Musset; L.42; (1980,1983)

Musique; for voice & piano;

Première Suite d'orchestre; for orchestra (also piano duet); L.50:
1) *Fête*; 2) *Ballet*; 3) *Rêve*; 4) *Bacchanale*

1884

En Sourdine; for voice & piano; first version; to Mme. Vasnier;
text by Paul Verlaine; L.28

Divertissement; for piano duet; L.36

Chansons de Jeunesse; for voice & piano; (1926, 1969):
1) *Pantomime*; 1883; text by Paul Verlaine; L.31; 2) *Clair
de Lune* (1st version); 1882; text by Paul Verlaine; L.32;
3) *Pierrot*; 1882; text by Théodor de Banville; L.15;
4) *Apparition*; text by Stephane Mallarmé; L.53

Chansons; for voice & piano; to Mme. Vasnier; mainly 1883/84;
texts by Paul Bourget unless otherwise stated; (1980; revised
1983): a) *Coquetterie posthume*; Théophile Gautier; L.39; b)
Chanson espagnole; Alfred de Musset; L.42; c) *Romance*; L.43; d)
Musique; L.44; e) *Romance d'Ariel*; L.54; f) *Paysage sentimentale*;
1883, revised 1891 & 1902; L.45; g) *Voici que le printemps*; 1884,
revised 1902; L.52; h) *Regret*; L.55

L'aimable printemps; for chorus & orchestra; text by Auguste
Barbier; L.56

L'Enfant prodigue; cantata; (winner of the Prix de Rome, 1884;
revised in 1906–08); to Ernest Guiraud; text by E. Guinand;
L.57; (1884; 1908)

1885

Barcarolle; for voice & piano; text by E. Guinand; L.58

Zuleima; for chorus; text by Augustin Boyer, after Heinrich
Heine; L.59

1886

Beau soir; for voice & piano; text by Paul Bourget; L.6; (1891)

Diane au bois; fragments of cantata; 1883–86; text by Théodor
    de Banville; L.51

Deux Romances; for voice & piano; texts by Paul Bourget; L.79;
    (1891): 1) *L'Âme évaporée*; 1884; 2) *Les cloches*; 1886

As You Like It; incidental music to William Shakespeare's play;
    never started

1887

Printemps; symphonic suite with chorus; 1887, revised 1912;
    to Auguste Durand; texts by M. Baschet 'after Botticelli';
    L.61; (1904, for piano; 1913, for orchestra)

1888

Ariettes oubliées; for voice & piano; to Mary Garden; texts by
    Paul Verlaine; L.60; (1888; revised versions 1903): 1) *C'est
    l'Extase langoureuse*; 1887; 2) *Il pleure dans mon coeur*; 1887;
    3) *L'Ombre des arbres*; 1885; 4) *Chevaux de bois*; 1885/87;
    5) *Green*; 1886; 6) *Spleen*; 1888

Axël; scenes towards an opera; text by Auguste Villiers de
    L'Isle-Adam; L.63

Cinq Poèmes de Charles Baudelaire; for voice & piano; texts by
    Baudelaire; L.64; (1890): 1) *Le Balcon*; 1888; 2) *Harmonie du
    Soir*; 1889; 3) *Le Jet d'eau*; 1889; (later orchestrated by
    Debussy & André Caplet); 4) *Recueillement*; 1889; 5) *La Mort
    des amants*; 1887

La Damoiselle élue; cantata; to Paul Dukas; 1887–88, revised in
    1902; text by Dante Gabriel Rossetti; L.62; (1893; 1903)

1889

Petite Suite; for piano duet; 1888–89; L.65; (1889):
    1) *En Bateau*; 2) *Cortège*; 3) *Menuet*; 4) *Ballet*

1890

Mazurka; for piano; 1890?; L.67; (1904)

Rêverie; for piano; L.68; (1895)

Danse; for piano; originally *Tarentelle styrienne*; L.69; (1891)

Ballade; for piano; originally *Ballade slave*; L.70; (1891, 1903)

Valse romantique; for piano; L.71; (1890)

Fantaisie; for piano & orchestra; 1889–90; L.73; (1920; revised
    1968)

La Belle au bois dormant; for voice & piano; text by E.-V. Hyspa;
  L.74; (1902)

1891

Deux Arabesques; for piano; 1888/91; L.66; (1891)

Les angélus; for voice & piano; text by G. Le Roy; L.76; (1891)

Marche écossaise sur un thème populaire; also first known as *Marche
  des anciens Comtes de Ross*; for piano duet; 1891, reworked 1903,
  orchestrated 1908; L.77; (1891 for piano, 1911 for orchestra)

Fêtes galantes; Set One; for voice & piano; second versions; first
  versions 1882; texts by Paul Verlaine; L.80; (1903):
  1) *En sourdine*; 2) *Fantoches*; 3) *Clair de Lune*

Trois Mélodies de Verlaine; for voice & piano; texts by Paul
  Verlaine; L.81; (1901): 1) *La Mer est plus belle*; 2) *Le Son du cor
  s'afflige*; 3) *L'Échelonnement des haies*

L'Embarquement pour ailleurs; incidental music to scenario by
  Gabriel Mourey; never started

La Princesse Maleine; opera to text by Maurice Maeterlinck,
  which Maeterlink refused

1892

Rodrigue et Chimène; opera; to Mlle. Gabrielle Dupont; text by
  Catulle Mendès; L.72.

Nocturne; for piano; L.82; (1892)

Trois Scènes au crépuscule; sketches for orchestra; (de Régnier);
  L.83

1893

Proses lyriques; for voice & piano; 1892–93; texts by Debussy;
  L.84; (1895): 1) *De rêve*; 2) *De grêve*; 3) *De fleurs*; 4) *De soir*

Quartet; for string quartet; to the Quatuor Ysaÿe; 1892–93;
  marked as 'Quartet No.1' and as 'Op.10'; L.85; (1894)

1894

Prélude à 'L'Après-midi d'un faune'; for orchestra; to Raymond
  Bonheur (later: to Gaby); 1892–94; (Stephane Mallarmé);
  L.86; (1895)

Images oubliées; for piano; L.87; (1977): 1) *Lent (mélancolique et
  doux)*; 2) *Souvenir du Louvre*; (1896); 3) *Quelques aspets de 'Nous
  n'irons plus au bois'*

Sonata; for violin & piano; never started
Quartet; for string quartet; never started
Valse; for piano; abandoned
Oedipe à Colonne; incidental music to Sophocles; abandoned
La Danseuse; ballet to scenario by Pierre Louÿs; abandoned

1895

Pelléas et Mélisande; opera; 1893–95, orchestration 1900–02;
    text by Maurice Maeterlinck; L.88; (1902, for piano; 1904,
    full score)
La grande bretèche; opera after Honoré de Balzac; never started

1896

Les Uns et les autres; opera; text by Paul Verlaine; never
    started
Salammbô; opera after Gustave Flaubert; abandoned
Orphée; ballet to scenario by Paul Valéry; never started

1897

Le Chevalier d'or; pantomime to scenario by Mme. J.-L. Forain;
    never started
Aphrodite; ballet to scenario by Pierre Louÿs; 1896–97; never
    started

1898

Chansons de Bilitis; for voice & piano; text by Pierre Louÿs; L.90;
    (1899): 1) *La Flûte de Pan*; 2) *La Chevelure*; 3) *Le Tombeau des
    naïades*
Two *Chansons de Charles d'Orléans*; see under 1908
Daphnis et Chloé; ballet to scenario by Pierre Louÿs; 1895–98;
    never started
Cendrelune; opera to text by Pierre Louÿs; never started

1899

Nocturnes; for orchestra; 1897–99; (related to *Trois Nocturnes*;
    for violin & orchestra; 1894–95); L.91; (1900; revised 1930;
    new revised 1964): 1) *Nuages*; 2) *Fêtes*; 3) *Sirènes* (with
    women's choir)
Berceuse (for *La Tragédie de la mort*); for solo voice; text by René
    Peter; L.93

1900

La Saulaie; fragments for baritone & orchestra; 1896–1900; text
  by Dante Gabriel Rossetti; L.89

1901

Pour le Piano; for piano; L.95; (1901); 1) *Prélude*; 2) *Sarabande*;
  1894–1901; 3) *Toccata*

Les Chansons de Bilitis; incidental music (completed by Arthur
  Hoérée & orchestrated by Pierre Boulez); texts by Pierre
  Louÿs; L.96; (1971): 1) *Chant pastorale*; (became *Épigraphes
  antiques*, No.1); 2) *Les Comparaisons*; 3) *Les Contes*; 4) *Chanson*;
  (became *Épigraphes antiques*, No.3); 5) *La Partie d'osselets*;
  6) *Bilitis*; 7) *Le Tombeau sans nom*; (became *Épigraphes antiques*,
  No.2); 8) *Les Courtisanes égyptiennes*; 9) *L'Eau pure du bassin*;
  10) *La Danseuse aux crotales*; (became *Épigraphes antiques*,
  No.4); 11) *Le Souvenir de Mnasidica*; 12) *La Pluie au matin*;
  (became *Épigraphes antiques*, No.6)

Lindaraja; for two pianos; L.97; (1926)

Le Voyage de Pausole; symphonic suite to text by Pierre Louÿs;
  abandoned

1902

La Damoiselle élue; cantata; revision of first version 1887–88;
  text by Dante Gabriel Rossetti; L.62; (1893; 1903)

Pelléas et Mélisande; opera; to Georges Hartmann & André
  Messager; 1893–95, orchestration 1900–02; text by Maurice
  Maeterlinck; L.88; (1902, for piano; 1904, full score)

Nuits blanches, 1 & 2; for voice & piano; 1899–1902; texts by
  Debussy; L.94; (1911)

As You Like It; incidental music to William Shakespeare's play;
  never started

1903

Ariettes oubliées; for voice & piano; revised versions; texts by
  Paul Verlaine; L.60; (1903)

Dans le Jardin; for voice & piano; text by P. Gravollet; L.78;
  (1905)

D'un Cahier d'esquisses; for piano; L.99; (1904)

Estampes; for piano; L.100; (1903): 1) *Pagodes*; 2) *La Soirée dans
  Grenade*; 3) *Jardins sous la pluie*

L'Isle joyeuse; for piano; L.106; (1904)

Briséis; projected completion of opera by Emmanuel Chabrier; not done

1904

Trois Chansons de France; for voice & piano; various texts; L.102; (1904): 1) *Le Temps a laissié son manteau*; Charles d'Orléans; 2) *La Grotte*; Tristan Lhermite; 3) *Pour ce que plaisance est morte*; Charles d'Orléans. (Nos.1 and 3 known also as *Rondel I & II*)

Deux Danses; for harp & string orchestra; L.103; (1904): 1) *Danse sacrée*; 2) *Danse profane*

Fêtes galantes; Set Two; for voice & piano; texts by Paul Verlaine; L.104; (1904): 1) *Les ingénus*; 2) *Le faune*; 3) *Colloque sentimental*

Masques; for piano; L.105; (1904)

Morceau de concours; for piano; L.108; (1905; 1980)

1905

Suite bergamasque; for piano; 1890–1905; L.75; (1905): 1) *Prélude*; 2) *Menuet*; 3) *Clair de lune*; 4) *Passepied*

La Mer; for orchestra; to Jacques Durand; 1903–05; L.109; (1905): a) *De l'Aube à midi sur la mer*; b) *Jeux de Vagues*; c) *Dialogue du Vent et de la mer*

Images; First Series; for piano; L.110; (1905): 1) *Reflets dans l'eau*; 2) *Hommage à Rameau*; 3) *Mouvement*

Valse; for two pianos; abandoned

1906

Musique pour 'Le roi Lear'; incidental music for orchestra; 1904–06; (William Shakespeare); L.107; (1926): 1) *Fanfare* (Overture); 2) *Le Sommeil de Lear*

1907

Images; Second Series; for piano; L.111; (1908): 1) *Cloches à travers les feuilles*; (Louis Laloy); 2) *Et la Lune descend sur le temple qui fut*; 3) *Poissons d'or*

1908

Trois Chansons de Charles d'Orléans; for 4 voices *a cappella*; texts by Charles d'Orléans; L.92; (1908): 1) *Dieu! qu'il la fait bon*

regarder; 1898; 2) *Quant j'ai ouy le tabourin*; 1908; 3) *Yver, vous n'estes qu'un villain*; 1898

Children's Corner; for piano; (also later orchestrated by André Caplet); to 'Chouchou'; 1908 unless otherwise marked; L.113; (1908): 1) *Doctor Gradus ad Parnassum*; 2) *Jimbo's Lullaby*; 3) *Serenade for the Doll*; 1906; 4) *The Snow is Dancing*; 5) *The Little Shepherd*; 6) *Golliwogg's Cakewalk* [sic]

L'Enfant prodigue; cantata; (first version 1884; revised in 1906–08); text by E. Guinand; L.57; (1884; 1908)

1909

The Little Nigar; for piano; L.114; (1909, 1934)

Hommage à Haydn; for piano; L.115; (1910)

L'Histoire de Tristan; opera never started, to text by Gabriel Mourey after Joseph Bédier

L'Orestie ; opera to text by Louis Laloy after Aeschylus; never started

Orphée-Roi; opera to text by Victor Segalen; never started

1910

Première Rapsodie; for clarinet & orchestra or piano; (competition piece for the Conservatoire); L.116; (1910)

Préludes; *Premier Cahier*; ('Book One'); for piano; mainly 1909–10; L.117; (1910): 1) *Danseuses de Delphes*; 2) *Voiles*; 3) *Le Vent dans la plaine*; (Charles-Simon Favart); 4) *Les Sons et les parfums tournent dans l'air du soir*; (Charles Baudelaire); 5) *Les Collines d'Anacapri*; 6) *Des Pas sur la neige*; 7) *Ce qu'a vu le Vent d'ouest*; (Anderson); 8) *La Fille aux cheveux de lin*; (Leconte de Lisle); (9) *La Sérénade interrompue*; 10) *La Cathédrale engloutie*; 11) *La Danse de Puck*; (William Shakespeare); 12) *Minstrels*

Le Promenoir des deux amants; for voice & piano; texts by Tristan Lhermite; L.118; (1910); 1) *Auprès de cette grotte sombre*; 1904; 2) *Crois mon conseil, chère Climène*; 1910; 3) *Je tremble en voyant ton visage*; 1910

Trois Ballades de Villon; for voice & piano; texts by François Villon; L.119; (1910): 1) *Ballade de Villon à s'ayme*; 2) *Ballade que Villon feit à la requeste de sa mère*; 3) *Ballade des femmes de Paris*

Petite pièce; for clarinet & piano; (competition piece for the Conservatoire); L.120; (1910)

La plus que lente; for piano; L.121; (1910)

Masques et Bergamasques; projected ballet abandoned; text by Debussy published 1910

Siddhartha; projected opera 1907–10, abandoned; text by Victor Segalen

1911

Rapsodie; for saxophone & orchestra; 1903–11; L.98; (1919)

Le Diable dans le beffroi; opera; 1902–11; text by Debussy after Edgar Allan Poe; L.101

Le Martyre de Saint Sébastien; ballet or incidental music for orchestra; text by Gabriele d'Annunzio; L.124; (1911)

Pygmalion; ballet after Jean Philippe Rameau; never started

La Dame à la faulx; incidental music to a scenario by Antoine Saint-Pol-Roux; never started

Ballet persan; ballet to scenario by Mme. P.-J. Toulet; abandoned

1912

Images pour orchestre; for orchestra; 1905–12; L.122; (1913): 1) *Gigues*; 1909–12; (originally *Gigues tristes*); 2) *Ibéria*; 1905–08; 3) *Rondes de printemps*; 1905–09

Préludes; *Deuxième Cahier*; ('Book Two'); for piano; mainly 1911–12; L.123; (1913): 1) *Brouillards*; 2) *Feuilles mortes*; 3) *La puerta del viño*; 4) *Les fées sont d'exquises danseuses*; (Arthur Rackham); 5) *Bruyères*; 6) *General Lavine – eccentric*; (General Lavine); 7) *La terrasse des audiences au clair de lune*; (R. Puaux); 8) *Ondine*; 9) *Hommage à S. Pickwick Esq. P.P.M.P.C.* (Charles Dickens); 10) *Canope*; 11) *Les tierces alternées*; 1913?; 12) *Feux d'artifice*; 1913?

Jeux; ballet for orchestra; scenario by Vaslav Nijinsky & Sergei Diaghilev; L.126; (1912)

Khamma; ballet for orchestra; orchestration by Debussy & Charles Koechlin; scenario by W.L. Courtney & Maude Allan; L.125; (1916, for piano)

Printemps; symphonic suite with chorus; revision of version of 1887; texts by Marcel Baschet 'after Botticelli'; L.61; (1904, for piano; 1913, for orchestra)

1913

Trois Poèmes de Stéphane Mallarmé; for voice & piano; to Stéphane

Mallarmé & Mme. E. Bonniot; texts by Stephane Mallarmé;
L.127; (1913): 1) *Soupir*; 2) *Placet futile*; 3) *Éventail*
La Boîte à joujoux; ballet for orchestra; L.128; (1913)
Syrinx; for solo flute; (only remaining part of work on *Psyché*, a
projected opera with text by Gabriel Mourey); L.129; (1927)

1914

No-ja-li; sketches for a ballet; includes *Le Palais du silence*;
scenario by Georges de Feure; L.130
Six Épigraphes antiques; for piano or piano duet; (mainly derived
from *Les Chansons de Bilitis*; 1901; texts by Pierre Louÿs);
L.131; (1915): 1) *Pour invoquer Pan, Dieu du vent d'été*;
2) *Pour un tombeau sans nom*; 3) *Pour que la nuit soit propice*;
4) *Pour la danseuse aux crotales*; 5) *Pour l'égyptienne*; 6) *Pour
remercier la pluie au matin*
Berceuse héroïque; for piano; L.132; (1914,1915)
Poème; for violin & orchestra; 1912–14; abandoned

1915

Page d'album; for piano; L.133; (1933, 1980)
En blanc et noir; three untitled movements for two pianos;
L.134; (1915)
Sonata; for cello & piano; to 'Chouchou'; L.135; (1915)
Études; in two books of six; for piano; to Frédéric Chopin;
L.136; (1916):
Book One: 1) *Pour les cinq doigts*; 2) *Pour les tierces*; 3) *Pour les
quatres*; 4) *Pour les sixtes*; 5) *Pour les octaves*; 6) *Pour les huit
doigts*
Book Two: 1) *Pour les degrés chromatiques*; 2) *Pour les agréments*;
3) *Pour les notes répétées*; 4) *Pour les sonorités opposées*; 5) *Pour les
arpèges composés*; 6) *Pour les accords*
Étude retrouvée; for piano; early version of No.11 of *Études* in
previous entry (Book Two, No.5); L.136*bis*; (1980)
Sonata; for flute, viola & harp; to 'Chouchou' L.137; (1915)
Élégie; for piano; L.138; (1916; 1978)
Noël des Enfants qui n'ont plus de maisons; for voice & piano; text
by Debussy; L.139; (1916)
Fêtes galantes; opera/ballet based on abandoned plans for *Crimen
amoris*, an opera to a text by Paul Verlaine; 1912?/1915; text
by Louis Laloy after Verlaine; L.Ann.IV

Sonatas; a) for oboe, horn & harpsichord; b) for trumpet, clarinet, bassoon & piano; c) for 'several instruments' & piano; all projected but never started

1917

La Chute de la maison Usher; opera; text by Debussy after Edgar Allan Poe; 1908–17; L.112; (1979)

Sonata; for violin & piano; to 'Chouchou'; L.140; (1917)

Ode à la France; for chorus; text by Louis Laloy; L.141; (1928)

Concerts; for piano & orchestra; never started

As You Like It ; incidental music to William Shakespeare's play; never started

SELECTED BIBLIOGRAPHY

There are several volumes of correspondence by Debussy, in French, but in English only one substantial volume has been compiled: **Debussy Letters**, edited by Lesure & Nichols (Faber & Faber, London, 1987). Roger Nichols has also compiled an interesting selection of other people's writings on Debussy: **Debussy Remembered** (Faber & Faber, London, 1992).

Debussy's journalism, **Monsieur Croche antidilettante**, was first issued in French in 1950 and first appeared in English in 1927, translated by N. Douglas. Another edition, edited by Lesure, came out in 1971 and in an enlarged edition in 1987 (Paris); the first edition was translated as **Debussy on Music**, edited and translated by R. L. Smith (London & New York, 1977).

Apart from letters, journalism, and some texts for his music, actual or projected, Debussy contributed a **Preface to an edition of Chopin's works** (Durand, Paris, 1915). Many of his friends – for instance Charles Koechlin, Louis Laloy, André Suarès and others – wrote souvenirs of the composer, but many appeared only in periodicals and few have been translated. The Roger Nichols anthology mentioned above provides an indispensible resource.

The standard English-language biography of Debussy is **Debussy: His Life and Mind**, by E. Lockspeiser (Dent, London, revised edition 1980). He also wrote a book entitled **Debussy**, in one volume (London, 1936, 1944, 1951, 1962, 1980).

Claude Debussy: His Life and Works, by L. Vallas (Dover, New York, 1973, from the French of 1932 & 1958), is not well presented nor always quite accurate, but is pleasingly written.

A Portrait of Claude Debussy, by M. Dietschy (Oxford University Press, Oxford, 1990), also not quite satisfactory, is nonetheless perhaps the most thorough recent Life in one volume.

Other books of interest on Debussy are:

Debussy, by J. Barraqué, translated by R. Troop (London, 1972)

Debussy and Wagner, by R. Holloway (Eulenberg, London, 1979)

Debussy in Proportion, by R. Howat (Cambridge & Boston, 1983)

Claude Debussy: The Story of His Life and Work, by R. Myers (London, 1972)

Debussy and the Theatre, by R. Orledge (Cambridge, 1982)

Index

THE
CLASSIC *f*M
GUIDE TO
CLASSICAL MUSIC

JEREMY NICHOLAS

'... *a fascinating and accessible guide ... it will provide
an informative and illuminating source of insight
for everybody from the beginner to the musicologist.*'

Sir Edward Heath

The Classic fM Guide to Classical Music opens with a masterly
history of classical music, illustrated with charts and lifelines, and
is followed by a comprehensive guide to more than 500 composers. There are major entries detailing the lives and works of the
world's most celebrated composers, as well as concise biographies
of more than 300 others.

This invaluable companion to classical music combines extensive
factual detail with fascinating anecdotes, and an insight into the
historical and musical influences of the great composers. It also
contains reviews and recommendations of the best works, and
extensive cross-references to lesser-known composers. Jeremy
Nicholas's vibrant, informative and carefully researched text is
complemented by photographs and cartoons, and is designed for
easy reference, with a comprehensive index.

£19.99   ISBN: 1 85793 760 0   **Hardback**
£9.99   ISBN: 1 86205 051 1   **Paperback**

CLASSIC *f*M
COMPACT COMPANIONS

CHOPIN, PUCCINI, ROSSINI, TCHAIKOVSKY

In association with *Classic fM* and *Philips Classics*, this revolutionary new series, *Compact Companions*, is a stylish package of book and compact disc. Each title provides the ultimate prelude to the lives and works of the most popular composers of classical music.

These composers' extraordinary, eventful lives and their powerful, moving music make them the ideal subjects for combined reading and listening. Written by respected authors, the texts provide a comprehensive introduction to the life and work of the composer, and each includes a richly illustrated biography, a complete list of works and a definitive list of recommended recordings. The accompanying CD combines both favourite and less-well-known pieces, recorded by artists of world renown.

Chopin
Christopher Headington
ISBN: 1 85793 655 8

Puccini
Jonathon Brown
ISBN: 1 85793 660 4

Rossini
David Mountfield
ISBN: 1 85793 665 5

Tchaikovsky
David Nice
ISBN: 1 85793 670 1

£9.99 (inc. VAT) each companion

These books can be ordered direct from the publisher.
Please contact the Marketing Department.
But try your bookshop first.

CLASSIC *f*M
LIFELINES

With 4.8 million listeners every week, *Classic fM* is now the most listened-to national commercial radio station in the UK. With the launch of *Classic fM Lifelines*, Pavilion Books and *Classic fM* are creating an affordable series of elegantly designed short biographies that will put everyone's favourite composers into focus.

Written with enthusiasm and in a highly accessible style, the ***Classic fM Lifelines*** series will become the Everyman of musical biographies. Titles for the series have been chosen from *Classic fM*'s own listener surveys of the most popular composers.

TITLES PUBLISHED:

Johannes Brahms
Jonathon Brown
ISBN: 1 85793 967 0

Claude Debussy
Jonathon Brown
ISBN: 1 85793 972 7

Edward Elgar
David Nice
ISBN: 1 85793 977 8

Gustav Mahler
Julian Haylock
ISBN: 1 85793 982 4

Sergei Rachmaninov
Julian Haylock
ISBN: 1 85793 944 1

Franz Schubert
Stephen Jackson
ISBN: 1 85793 987 5

£4.99 each book

FORTHCOMING TITLES:

- ◆ *J.S. Bach*
- ◆ *Ludwig van Beethoven*
- ◆ *Benjamin Britten*

- ◆ *Joseph Haydn*
- ◆ *Dmitri Shostakovich*
- ◆ *Ralph Vaughan Williams*

CLASSIC *f*M
LIFELINES

To purchase any of the books in the *Classic fM Lifelines* series
simply fill in the order form below and post or fax it,
together with your remittance, to the address below.

Please send the titles ticked below
(*published spring 1997)

Johannes Brahms	☐	*J.S. Bach	☐
Claude Debussy	☐	*Ludwig van Beethoven	☐
Edward Elgar	☐	*Benjamin Britten	☐
Gustav Mahler	☐	*Joseph Haydn	☐
Sergei Rachmaninov	☐	*Dmitri Shostakovich	☐
Franz Schubert	☐	*Ralph Vaughan Williams	☐

Number of titles @ £4.99 _____   Value: £_____

Add 10% of total value for postage and packing   Value: £_____

Total value of order: £_____

I enclose a cheque (UK only) payable to Pavilion Books Ltd ☐

OR

Please charge my credit card account ☐

I wish to pay by: Visa ☐ MasterCard ☐ Access ☐ American Express ☐

Card number ☐☐☐☐☐☐☐☐☐☐☐☐☐☐☐☐☐☐

Signature_____   Expiry Date_____

Name_____

Address_____

_____ Postcode_____

Please send your order to: Marketing Department, Pavilion Books Ltd,
26 Upper Ground, London SE1 9PD, or fax for quick dispatch to:
Marketing Department, 0171-620 0042.